Doing Business in India: Selected Themes to Consider

Doing Business in India:
Selected Themes to Consider

Edited by
Jan Stentoft
Ole Stegmann Mikkelsen
Antony Paulraj

University Press of Southern Denmark

2014

© The authors and University Press of Southern Denmark
Printed by Grafisk Produktion Odense ApS

ISBN: 978-87-91070-88-4

University Press of Southern Denmark
Campusvej 55
5230 Odense M
Denmark
www.universitypress.dk

Table of Content

Preface	**5**
Introduction	11
Organising the trip	13
Travel plan	13
The thank yous	14
Chapter 1 - Prologue: Why Study Business in India?	**15**
Abstract	15
Introduction	15
General information about India	16
Geography	17
History	18
Population	19
Language	20
Religion and caste	21
Economic development in India	22
Economic development in Tamil Nadu	24
Chapter 2 - Indian Business Culture	**25**
Abstract	25
Introduction	25
Research questions	27
Methodology	27
Literature review	28
Power distance	28
Collectivism versus individualism	33
Uncertainty avoidance	37
Masculinity versus femininity	40
Long term versus short term orientation	43
Implications	47

Conclusion ... 50

Chapter 3 - Innovation in India ... 53

Abstract ... 53

Introduction ... 53

Research questions ... 54

Literature review ... 54

   Drivers for innovation ... 57

Methodology ... 58

Drivers for innovation ... 59

   Political/regulatory drivers ... 59

   Socio-cultural drivers ... 60

   Technological drivers ... 61

   Economic drivers ... 62

   Part conclusion ... 63

Analysis of the case companies ... 64

   Process innovation ... 64

   Product ... 65

   Paradigm ... 66

   Inclusive innovation ... 67

   Cross company analysis ... 68

   Part conclusion ... 71

Other factors regarding innovation ... 71

   From where do innovations originate? ... 72

   Product innovation reflection ... 73

   Process innovation reflection ... 74

   Paradigm innovation reflection ... 75

   What influences a creative climate ... 76

   Part conclusion ... 78

Conclusion ... 79

Chapter 4 - Knowledge Management 83

Abstract 83
Introduction 83
Methodology 84
The Knowledge Management concept 85
Sharing knowledge 86
The importance of transforming tacit knowledge into explicit knowledge 89
Cultural distance in relation to knowledge sharing 91
The importance of Knowledge Management when sourcing to India 93
    Sharing knowledge from a Danish company to an Indian company 95
    Use of knowledge in the Indian companies 97
The personalisation perspective 98
    Using expatriates - understanding of expatriates in a HRM perspective 98
    Organisational structure and absorptive capacity 100
The codification perspective 103
    Building a successful knowledge-base 103
    IT-systems as tools for knowledge sharing 104
        Data warehousing 104
        Data mining 105
        Content management systems (CMS) 105
        ERP and CRM systems 105
    Implementation of IT-systems for knowledge sharing 106
        Focus on the Knowledge Management strategy 107
        The support of Human Resource Management 108
        Implementing IT-based Knowledge Management systems 109
Conclusion 111

Chapter 5 - Outsouring or Offshoring? 113

Abstract 113
The drivers for globalisation 113

Definitions	115
Literature review	115
OLIE	115
Ownership-specific advantages	116
Location-specific advantages	116
Internalisation vs. externalisation advantages	117
PESTEL	118
Delimitation	119
Methodology	119
The two companies	120
How to maintain the owner specific advantages	120
Owner specific advantages for the manufacturing company	120
Owner specific advantages for the knowledge company	122
An overview of the owner specific advantages	123
India as a market for Danish companies	124
Political	125
Economics	126
Social and cultural	128
Technological	128
Environmental	128
Challenges and advantages in India	129
Location challenges	129
Location-specific advantages	131
Choosing a globalisation strategy	133
Resume	135
OLIE model – the right way to go?	136
Conclusion	136
Chapter 6 - Epilogue: Learning af Reflection	**139**
Abstract	139

Introduction	139
Most impressive experiences	140
Application of relevant theories and methods	141
Improved competencies through group work	142
Better understanding of Indian culture	143
The most important points of cultural learning	144
Conclusion	145
Indian business culture	145
Innovation in India	146
Knowledge Management	146
Outsourcing or offshoring?	147
List of References	**149**
Index	**161**
About the Editors	**163**
Previous Field Study Projects	163

PREFACE

Introduction

This book, entitled "Doing Business in India: Selected Themes to Consider", contains 16 students' answers to assignments related to a study trip to India in the period of 5th October to 12th of October 2013. The study trip was part of the optional subject "International field studies" at Master of Science (MSc) in Business Administration at the Department of Entrepreneurship and Relationship Management, University of Southern Denmark, Kolding.

The purpose of the field study optional subject is, in general, to develop the student's skills to apply specific theories and analysis tools to a general philosophy of science and methodological perspective in actual business problem areas. Furthermore, it is a purpose that the students acquire experience with the requirements of international field studies regarding technical as well as social competencies. The aim of the course is to train the students to conduct all phases and facets within a smaller field study including the preparatory desk research part, organisation of the field work and later follow-up analysis and reports.

In the present context, this field study aims to achieve a general knowledge as to doing business and from a Western perspective to outline challenges that should be taken into account, when trading with India. More specifically, the students have examined fields of study within four topic areas:

1. Indian Business Culture
2. Innovation in India
3. Knowledge Management
4. Outsourcing or Offshoring?

The first topic, "Indian Business Culture" has been chosen because an understanding of cultural differences is perceived as being the overriding success criteria for doing business in India. The theme of innovation has been included to focus on Indian innovation capabilities in order to provide a deeper understanding of how Indians perceive and operate with the concept of innovation. The third theme is about knowledge management in connection with sourcing business processes from India. The last chapter is concerned with outsourcing and offshoring as means to start-up businesses in India from abroad.

The students have discussed theory and collected data related to the above four topics. In order to be able to report the findings to the companies, it was necessary to write the assignments in English. Furthermore, to increase the ambition level of the assignments, we decided to contact the University Press of Southern Denmark for an agreement to publish the assignments. The students responsible for each of the four book chapters are listed in Table 1.

Table 1: Students divided into the four themes

Indian Business Culture	Innovation in India	Knowledge Management	Outsourcing or Offshoring?
Janni Haahr Larsen	Maria Sudarschini Yogasundram	Henriette Kolbeck Thorsten Søgaard Krægpøth	Jeanette Holm Mette Husum Dalstrup
Rikke Wilhelmsen	Tina Møller Jensen		
Victoria Natali	Ena Cerimagic	Lasse Skov	
Electra Baagøe-Engels	Jesper Amstrup Hjelt	Christopher Wulff	
Mathias Lenholdt	Louise Beck Jochumsen		
Mathilde Tranbjerg Vammen			

The students are studying MSc in Management and Leadership, MSc in International Business Development and MSc in Business Controlling. The MSc line in Management and Leadership is structured around two central competence areas. The managing part provides knowledge and tools for solving problems regarding SCM, operations management and management accounting. The focus is on the roles and functions in global supply chains and the basic operation systems and philosophies (Just-In-Time, Lean, Agility etc.). The leadership part ensures understanding of and competence in solving problems within leadership, organisational changes and strategy development.

The MSc line in International Business Development sets focus on the interaction between organisations, be it private companies or public organisations. Specifically, information on international business and market development is communicated as well as insight into theories concerning companies' international business development, marketing and organisation.

Insight is gained into factors that influence the organisational change processes of the companies and the management of these processes. Whether the area is purchase or sale of products or projects to be carried through in a public environment, a number of different employees will be involved in the interaction between two or more organisations. The understanding of the interaction between individuals with different professional and cultural background is considered the key to successful company management.

The MSc line in Business Controlling develops a detailed insight into advanced audit theories, audit methods and techniques that are applied in both national and international oriented companies and their supply chains. The students obtain business understanding in order to explore and exploit IT systems to control activities and resource consumption in companies. Furthermore, the students obtain operational problem solving capabilities within operations management and management accounting that are useful when working with development oriented issues of companies' strategic development.

Organising the trip

First of all it should be mentioned that the students planned this study trip themselves. There has been a planning period of about 8 months with identifying, contacting and setting up appointments with companies, fundraising, providing communication about the study trip, organising flights and hotels, transportation to and from companies and sightseeing. In order to solve these tasks the students organised into different working groups with a representative in a steering group.

Travel plan

The field study trip in 2013 included visits in Chennai. The field study trip began October 7th with a visit at the Danish Consulate in Chennai in which all groups of students participated. The following four days we visited BWE, Rambøll, Vestas, Danfoss FLSmidth, El-Forge, Caresoft and Ramsay's.

The thank yous

Many persons have contributed to making this study trip possible. We will therefore thank these people and organisations for their support (time, knowledge and financial support). The persons and organisations are mentioned below.

Funding
Ole Kirks Fond
The business economy staff-student committee, University of Southern Denmark, Kolding

Companies that have been visited
SB Prabhakar Rao, The Danish Consulate in Chennai
Partha Sarathi Banik, BWE
Anders R. Knudsen, Gayathr iShankar and Balaji Swaminathan, Rambøll
Henrik Ib Jensen & Rengarajan Srinivasan, Vestas
Henrik Schurmann, Danfoss
Jesper B. Larsen, FLSmidth
Sri Hari, El-forget
Arjun Nagendra, Caresoft
R. Krishnakumar, Ramsay's

This book would not have been possible without the financial support of one company. Therefore we thank Tresu Production Systems A/S for financial support. We also would like to thank PhD student Christopher Rajkumar for his help with data included in chapter 1 and Department Secretary Ingeborg Uldahl for light proof reading.

Finally, we would like to thank the students for a well-organised field study trip and for their proactive learning attitude. Beyond excelling in company visits with discussions and factory tours, they contributed with events to make this trip also a fun experience. We certainly believe that this trip has been a learning experience for the students - technically, socially and culturally.

Best regards and hopefully enjoyable reading.
September 2014

Jan Stentoft	Ole Stegmann Mikkelsen	Antony Paulraj
Professor, PhD	Assistant Professor, PhD	Professor, PhD

CHAPTER 1

Prologue: Why study Business in India?

Antony Paulraj, Jan Stentoft & Ole Stegmann Mikkelsen

Abstract

Since its economic liberalisation in 1991, India has seen a considerable growth in its economy. In fact, the Indian economy has continued to grow steadily between 4 and 8 percent every year. Additionally, a number of factors – including greater percentage of its population being employable, growing middle class, exploding domestic market and continued economic growth – make India an interesting context. Accordingly, in this book, we investigate the climate of doing business in India. Specifically, taking a global supply chain perspective, we aspire to answer questions such as how does Indian culture differ from Danish culture? How does innovation take place in India? Before delving into these questions, we dedicate this prologue to not only give some details revolving around the history and demographics of this intriguing country, but also to set the stage for unravelling our experience and answers pertaining to the research questions.

Introduction

Though India has had a long-standing historical presence in the world (for 4 to 5 centuries), its economic stature had been significantly battered owing to multiple invasions from the west. Accordingly, during its independence in 1947 and the ensuring decades, India was positioned as an underdeveloped nation. Moreover, for many years after its independence, India had one of the most protected and regulated economies in the world (Kotwal et al., 2011). But the economic liberalisation act has changed this trend and has put India on a trajectory of steep economic progress (Pagadala and Mulaik, 2009).

Though India is a single country, it compares very much to Europe. Given that almost every state within India has its own language and culture,

Indian states can be compared to the different countries within Europe. India is the personification of the sentiment "Unity in Diversity" as it embodies multiple languages (with multiple dialects within each language), religions, cultures, clothing and food. One of the fundamental understandings for firms aspiring to do business in India is that they have to understand and appreciate this diversity.

India is the second most populous nation in the world, only next to China. The positive side of this story is that the majority of this population is young; this gives India the unique opportunity of having the world's largest employable population in many years to come. More importantly, the Indian youth is highly motivated and well trained in professional disciplines such as engineering, law and medicine. This, in addition to the significant growth in the service and manufacturing sectors, provides India with the opportunity to effectively compete against leading economies such as the United States and China into the distant future.

Another interesting aspect of India is its growing middle class. The level of disposable income in these families is increasingly enabling them to aspire for as well as lead a Western lifestyle. Accordingly, there is a large domestic market for goods and services offered by multinational companies. The simultaneous presence of high potential workforce and market opportunities makes India an ideal place for setting up businesses that could not only serve the world market, but also the local Indian market.

General information about India

India, a country in South Asia, was originally known as the Republic of India (*Bharatiya Ganarajya*). Often touted as a country which personifies the notion of "unity in diversity", India stands as the largest constitutional democratic country in the world. The Indian government has both a President and a Prime Minister. The President is the formal head of the legislative, executive, as well as judiciary branches of the Indian government and is also the commander in chief of the Indian Armed Forces. The 13th and current President Pranab Mukherjee was elected to office on 22 July 2012. As per the Indian constitution, the Prime Minister is the chief of government and leads the executive branch. The 15th and current Prime Minister Narendra Modi was elected to office on 26 May 2014. He is the leader of the Bharatiya Janata Party (BJP) and hails from the state of Gujarat. The Parliament of India (Bharatiya Sansad) is the supreme legislative body. It comprises two houses – House of the People (Lok Sabha) and Council of States (Rajya Sabha). While the Lok Sabha has a maximum strength of 545 seats, the Rajya Sabha has a maximum strength of 250 seats. The central government is situated in New Delhi, the capital of India. The Supreme Court of India is the highest judicial body, highest constitutional court, as well as the guardian of the constitution. The highest ranking judge of the Supreme Court of India is the Chief Justice of India. The 41st and current Chief Justice is Rajendra Mal Lodha.

Geography

India occupies most of the Indian subcontinent, which is a peninsula surrounded by three oceans – Bay of Bengal, Indian Ocean and the Arabian Sea. Accordingly, India has a long coastline which measures to about 7,000 kilometres and boasts the second longest beach in the world, Marina Beach. It is the 7th largest country in the world and is situated north of the Equator. With a total area of 3,287,263 sq. kilometres, it is more than 75 times larger than Denmark. Apart from being surrounded by three oceans, India also shares land borders with many Asian countries including Pakistan, China, Bangladesh, and Nepal (CIA World Factbook, 2014). India has a diverse landscape including rugged mountains, plains, as well as plateaus. Additionally, apart from housing the Thar dessert, India is also famous for the wettest place in the world, Cherrapunji. As for natural resources, India has the 4th largest coal reserves in the world. It also has deposits of important minerals such as iron, bauxite, diamonds, limestone, etc. (CIA World Factbook, 2014).

At the time being, the country is divided into 29 states and 7 union territories (Government of India, 2014). Since our study trip was focused on Chennai which is the state capital of Tamil Nadu, we provide some additional information about this state. Tamil Nadu is the 11th largest state in India with an area of 130,058 sq. kilometres. The state has the 3rd longest coastline in India and boasts the Marina beach (the second longest beach in the world). The state's water resources are heavily dependent on monsoon rains – the south-west monsoon from June to September and the north-east monsoon from October to December each year. The climate of the state ranges from sub-humid to semi-arid.

Just like any other country in the world, India is also prone to some localised natural disasters. Therefore, when doing business in India, individuals and organisations must be aware of the fact that depending on your location in India one could encounter hazards such as droughts, floods due to monsoon rains, cyclones, thunderstorms, and earthquakes. Additionally, businesses should also be aware of some environmental problems that are prevalent in India such as deforestation, soil erosion, air and water pollution from effluents as well as emissions, and, more importantly, overstraining of natural resources due to increasing population (CIA World Factbook, 2014).

History

India has a rich and long-standing history that dates back to the Indus Valley civilisation of the 3rd millennium BC. The original inhabitants of India were called Dravidians who were well known for their commerce and agriculture trade. Given its richness in natural resources, India was invaded by many Aryan tribes. The Aryan invasion pushed the Dravidian tribes to the south; Dravidian culture still remains the strongest in the state of Tamil Nadu that was visited by our group. The Persian and Greek invasions started as early as 5th century BC. The Mauryan Empire (4th to 3rd centuries BC) was one of the geographically extensive Empires that united ancient India into one state. Some of the prominent Mauryan Emperors were Chandragupta Maurya and Ashoka the Great. Even during the periods of these great kingdoms, the southern part of India held against this invasion. This part was ruled by Tamil (Dravidian) kings. Some of the prominent South Indian dynasties were Chola, Chera, Pandya, and Pallava dynasties. The next prominent empire of the northern part of India was the Gupta Empire. This period was also referred to as the Golden Age of India as it marked significant achievements in the fields of science, medicine, engineering, mathematics, astronomy and philosophy.

The next few centuries saw incursions from Islamic rulers (e.g., Mughals). After Vasco da Gama discovered a new sea route from Europe to India in the 15th century, European traders and colonists – Portuguese, Dutch, British, and French – began setting up trading posts in India. The internal feuds among the Indian kingdoms helped the European colonists to gradually establish their political influence in India. Eventually, the British Empire took control of majority of India by the 19th century. From 1920, freedom fighters including "Mahatma" Mohandas Gandhi began non-violent movements to campaign against the British rule. Through non-violent methods like non-cooperation, civil disobedience, and economic resistance, these freedom fighters led by Gandhi succeeded in getting independence for India. In 1947, the subcontinent was separated into two countries – India and Pakistan; in 1971, a war between India and Pakistan resulted in the Eastern part of Pakistan becoming Bangladesh.

Subsequent to its independence, India faced numerous problems including religious violence, naxalism, and terrorism. Even to date, India has unresolved territorial disputes with China and Pakistan. India conducted its first democratic elections in 1952. India is now recognised as a nuclear-weapon state. India has also evidenced significant economic development. It is also seen as major world power with a significant say in global affairs. In spite of such recognition, India still faces major road blocks when it comes to population, poverty, and corruption (CIA World Factbook, 2014).

Population

The current population of India is about 1,210 billion as per the official census conducted in 2011 (17.5 of the world population). According to unofficial 2014 estimates, Indian population is around 1,236 billion (CIA World Factbook, 2014). India is only one of the two countries with population above 1 billion and it is ranked second after China. Even though the rate of population in India has slowed significantly in recent years, a report by UN suggests that India will surpass China by 2028 (The Times of India, 2013).

When compared to USA and Europe, Indian population seems to be skewed more towards the younger age groups (see Table 1.1).

Table 1.1: Indian population by age (2011 census)

Age Group	Percentage
0-14 yrs.	28.5
15-24 yrs.	18.1
25-64 yrs.	40.6
65 + yrs.	5.7

Source: CIA World Factbook (2014)

According to the official census of 2011, more than 50 percent of the Indian population is below the age of 25 years.

A majority of the Indian population (approximately 69 percent) still lives in rural areas. But there is a constant movement of the rural population to urban areas. The urbanisation rate currently stands at 2.47 percent (CIA World Factbook, 2014).

Another key population statistics relates to the size of middle class people in India. This number has been growing at a faster rate and is expected to reach 267 million by 2015-2016 (The Economic Times, 2011). Similarly, the literacy rate has also been on the incline with the current rate being at around 62 percent. But when compared to men (75 percent), the literacy rate of women is estimated to be considerably lower (51 percent) (CIA World Factbook, 2014).

Another glaring problem that is evident when looking at the latest 2011 Indian official census is that the male-female ratio gap has been quite consistent in the past decade. As of now, there are 940 females for every 100 females.

Finally, India is prone to high degree of risk when it comes to major infectious diseases that are foodborne, waterborne, vector-borne, as well as those caused by contact with animals (CIA World Factbook, 2014). Still, with the increase in life expectancy rates, these major infections do not seem to have any significant impact on the rate of population growth.

Language

According to the first comprehensive linguistic survey conducted by the People's Linguistic Survey of India in 2013, there are 780 different languages currently spoken in India. These languages actually use 86 different scripts (The Hindustan Times, 2013). The number of languages also attributes to the diversity that is evident in India. In effect, every state within India has its own set of languages, which often are based on their own script. Therefore, even though there are many official languages in India, English can be considered as the most important common language of communication among individuals, businesses, and government entities. The diversity in language and the fact that most schools adopt English as the primary language has led Indians to be more proficient in English in comparison to inhabitants of other prominent Asian countries (e.g. China). Table 1.2 lists the top five languages in terms of the percentage of people who consider them as their mother tongue.

Table 1.2: Top five languages in India (2001 census)

Language	Percentage
Hindi	41.0
Bengali	8.1
Telugu	7.2
Marathi	7.0
Tamil	5.9

Source: CIA World Factbook, 2014

Religion and caste

The Indians follow many different religions such as Hinduism, Islam, Christianity, Buddhism and Sikhism. In fact, world's dominant religions such as Hinduism, Buddhism, Jainism and Sikhism have their origin in India. Historically, Indians have always been devout practitioners of whichever religion they followed. Every day, you can see a multitude of Indians visit and worship at temples, churches as well as mosques. The common man is actually very tolerant of other religious practices and does not hesitate to visit shrines of other religions. As evident from Table 1.3, Hindus make up the majority in India; every other religion is considered a minority.

Table 1.3: Religion in India (based on 2001 census)

Religion	Percentage
Hindus	80.5
Muslims	13.4
Christians	2.3
Sikhs	1.9
Buddhists	0.8
Jauns	0.4
Other	0.6

Source: Indian Census Bureau (2014)

Unlike religions such as Christianity and Islam that portray one God, Hinduism consists of multiple Gods. But the three prime Gods are Brahma (the Creator), Vishnu (the Protector), and Shiva (the Destructor). In addition, there are also some regional Gods such as Muruga (Tamil Nadu) and Ayyappa (Kerala). While religion-based conflicts happen intermittently, such conflicts are not that prevalent in the southern part of the country.

Apart from religion, Indians are also segregated based on the caste system, a system of social stratification. Though the origin of the caste system is unclear, it is still quite prevalent in most parts of India. The four main castes in India (Brahmin, Kshatriya, Vaishya, and Shudra) closely mirror that of the Aryan classes or pistras (Priests, Warriors, Merchants, and Artisans). The Indian government strives to elevate the stature of discriminated communities such as the scheduled caste and scheduled tribe (previously referred to as untouchables) through special reservation (affirmative action) policies in education and jobs.

Economic development in India

As part of the BRIC nations, India is part of a select group of developing countries that has the economic potential to rank among the most influential economies in the 21st century. Specifically, if it sustains its current growth rate, India has the potential of becoming the third largest economy in the world by 2050 (Global Sherpa, 2014; Shiralashetti and Hugar, 2009). Additionally, India is considered as one of the top economies in the world in terms of purchasing power parity as well as gross domestic product (CIA World Factbook, 2014). As indicated earlier, this economic growth was the result of the economic liberalisation policy that was initiated in 1991 by the then Prime Minister Narasimha Rao and Finance Minister Manmohan Singh.

Fuelled by this open market economic policy, the Indian economy has grown between four and eight percent every year since the mid-1990s. While the past two years have seen a mild decline in the growth rate, the 2014-2015 first quarter's economic growth of 5,7 percent has indicated that India is back on its impressive increasing growth trajectory (The Hindu, 2014). In general, this economic growth could be attributed to economic policies of the country as well as the individual states, market reforms, increasing flow of foreign direct investments (FDI), manufacturing and service industry boom, and the expanding local markets. In light of its potential in becoming a prominent economy of the future, India has been inducted into both the G20 and the World Trade Organisation.

Taking a closer look at the drivers of the Indian economic growth, it is evident that agriculture, service and the manufacturing industries play a prominent role in the development of the Indian economy. As for agriculture, it accounts for 14 percent of the country's GDP and 11 percent of its exports (Government of India, 2013). India is the second largest in terms of the world's agricultural output (Economy Watch, 2010). The robustness of the agriculture industry is fuelled by improvements in irrigation processes, adoption of modern technologies, and ongoing research and development carried out by research institutions in India (Economy Watch, 2010). In 2009, the agricultural sector employed more than 50 percent of the total work force. However, a recent survey conducted by the National Council for Applied Economic Research shows that there is a considerable decline in agriculture employment (The Hindu, 2014).

When it comes to the manufacturing output, India is ranked 14th in the world (Economy Watch, 2010). More importantly, when it comes to manufacturing competence, a report by Deloitte indicates that India is ranked second in the world, ahead of USA and South Korea (The Economic Times, 2010). Given its superior research prowess, engineering design and development capabilities, English-speaking workforce, and more importantly, democratic government, the report also hints to the fact that India will have strong foothold on this position well into the future. Some of the flourishing industries in the manufacturing sector are the automobile and electronics industries. Other industries such as gas, mining, electricity also contribute to the Indian GDP considerably (Economy Watch, 2010).

Last, but not the least, the growth in the Indian service sector has been the most successful story. Even before its manufacturing prowess, the world recognised India for its prowess within the service industry. Especially, companies in information technology, software development, business process outsourcing, and knowledge process outsourcing have been the biggest contributors within the service sector. A recent Indian economic survey indicates that India has the second fastest growing services sector (rate of nine percent), second only to China (The Hindu, 2014). This report also indicates that the software services export accounts for 46 percent of India's total services exports.

While the future looks promising for the Indian economy, it is not free of potential barriers. One of the key issues facing the Indian economy is the inflation rate. As per the Worldwide Inflation Data (2014), the inflation rate in India is currently at 7,23 percent. This can cause undue pressure on wages and prices within India, two major issues that might impede its global competitiveness when it comes to the service and manufacturing sectors. Another major economic threat is poverty. According to the Rangarajan committee reports, 29,5 percent of the Indian population is below the poverty line (set at those spending Rs. 32 per day in rural areas and Rs. 47 in urban areas) (The Times of India, 2014). But through its national and regional initiatives, the government of India is striving to address the needs of the poor, as eliminating poverty will be important for the future development of the country.

Economic development in Tamil Nadu

As illustrated earlier, India is not only a large country in terms of size and population, but is also a country of diversities in language, religion, ethnicity, and most importantly, economic growth. Since we visited the city of Chennai in Tamil Nadu, we provide specific details regarding the economic developments in this south Indian state.

In spite of being the 11th largest state in the nation, the State of Tamil Nadu is the second most industrialised state. More importantly, it is placed third in attracting FDIs within the country; in the period 2011-2012, the state attracted around Rs. 6.711 crores, which is around 66 percent higher than its neighbouring state of Andhra Pradesh (Business Standard, 2014). The state attracts increasing amounts from FDI by setting up industrial parks and special economic zones that offer significant tax incentives to foreign entities.

The state is well known for its dominant service as well as manufacturing sectors. In the manufacturing sector, the state is known for its agriculture, engineering, auto components, textiles, leather, sugar, etc. (Tamil Nadu Online, 2014). In fact, many heavy engineering and automotive companies are located in and around Chennai, which is popularly dubbed as the "Detroit of South-east Asia". Many leading global auto manufacturing giants like Hyundai, Ford, BMW, Daimler and Renault have their assembly plants in this metropolitan city. Chennai has also emerged as a leading hub for leather and electronics industry. The textile industry also plays a significant role in the state by contributing to almost 14 percent of the manufacturing sector (Tamil Nadu Online, 2014).

CHAPTER 2

Indian Business Culture

Janni Haahr Larsen, Rikke Wilhelmsen, Victoria Natali Electra Baagøe-Engels, Mathias Lenholdt & Mathilde Tranbjerg Vammen

Abstract

The purpose of this chapter is to describe the cultural issues that Danish companies should be aware of when doing business in India. India is a diverse culture and this chapter attempts to combine different cultural theories with the practical field trip in order to set some common guidelines for cooperating with Indian companies. It was found that the Indian culture differs from the Danish, especially in terms of power distance, collectivism versus individualism, masculinity versus femininity and long term versus short term orientation. However, in relation to uncertainty avoidance the difference is minor.

Introduction

The overall topic of the book 'Doing Business in India' welcomes a lot of opportunities for different research areas. In this chapter we will focus on culture and the attention will be pointed towards the cultural barriers which occur when two different cultures engage in business cooperation. Danish companies entering the Indian market encounter various challenges, among which the cross-cultural cooperation between the firms and their employees is a central concern. The focus of this chapter will therefore be to explore the cultural differences between Danish and Indian business culture, which is of great importance for Danish companies in order to be successful in the corporation with India.

In relation to the evolvement of the international market and the evolvement of business cooperation between different countries, the cultural differences and especially the cultural adaptation between two cooperating companies have always been an important factor. Without the proper understanding and a clear knowledge of the differences between one's own culture and a foreign culture, the art of doing business will be complicated for Danish companies. As the global market place becomes increasingly smaller every day, the cultural issues are becoming a more pressing matter. Even though failures might occur due to lack of cultural knowledge, some trends indicate that two geographically spread countries like Denmark and India also follow the global evolution when you talk of culture. Despite of the fact that the world market is getting smaller and cultural insight is getting bigger, there are still cultural misunderstandings and adaption failures that cost the companies both money and resources.

Hofstede refers to this as a *"cultural shock"* (Hofstede and Hofstede, 2006, p. 341), because individuals have a set of values that are unique for the specific culture they are a part of. Specifically, when dealing with business cultures and especially the combination of two different cultures, Gesteland appoints the importance of understanding your business partner's culture in order to make the best deal, and furthermore stresses that it is the responsibility of the visitor to observe local customs (Gesteland, 2005, p. 18). This supports the importance of Danish business companies' understanding of the cultures in which they engage for business purposes. This research focuses on the business cooperation between Danish and Indian companies. The difference between the two cultures is significant according to both Hofstede and Gesteland. According to Hofstede the Indian culture, among other things, is based on a high power distance, whereas the Danish culture is based on a low power distance (Hofstede and Hofstede, 2006, p. 59). The Indian culture is based on a collectivistic culture, whereas the Danish culture is based on an individualistic point of view (Hofstede and Hofstede, 2006, p. 94). Furthermore, when taking Gesteland's point of view, the Danish business culture is deal-focused, moderately formal and monochromic, whereas the Indian culture is focused on relationship, formal, polychronic and reserved (Gesteland, 2005, p. 125 ff. and 279 ff.).

With this chapter, Danish companies will get an insight into the cultural barriers that might occur when cooperating with India. Having this cultural knowledge Danish companies are able to anticipate cultural conflicts and prevent using unnecessary resources. The benefits of this chapter for Danish companies will be further outlined during the chapter and summarised in the final section concerning implications.

This leads to the next section of this chapter in which we will present the specific research questions that have been found relevant in relation to doing business in India and specifically the cooperation between Danish and Indian companies.

Research questions

The above-mentioned subjects lead to the introduction of the overall research theme, which is clearly stated as *"Cultural differences between Denmark and India in a business perspective"*. The following research questions will help cover the overall research theme:

- *How do Indian employees react with regard to a formal hierarchy structure within the company?*
- *To which degree is the Indian society collectivistic or individualistic?*
- *In what way does the Indian society control uncertainty regarding the future?*
- *Which values define the Indian society?*
- *To what degree does time matter in the Indian society?*

It should be noted that the research questions only concern the business context. A study of the whole society would indeed be interesting, although less appropriate. This book is aimed at business people who want to know about the Indian business culture; therefore a business approach is the right choice.

Methodology

The preparations for this book chapter started before the field trip to India. The reason for this was to prepare a theoretical framework in order to sustain and understand key factors regarding culture. The pre-research consisted of various articles and literature studies. After a literature review a semi structured questionnaire was prepared to be used during the visits to the different companies. The empirical research included a total of nine companies in Chennai, six of which were Danish subsidiaries. These six companies will be referred to as global companies (Company A-F), whereas the remaining companies with origin in India will be referred to as domestic (Company X-Z). It was arranged that the companies received the questionnaire in advance in order for them to prepare. The companies began the visit with an introduction of their company, which lead to a further elaboration on the questions, in order to gather the necessary data. All companies were represented by different managers, which resulted in a deep understanding of the company and business culture in India.

Literature review

Many different researchers have contributed to the study of cultural barriers that may be encountered when combining two different cultures. This chapter will focus primarily on Geert Hofstede, a Dutch social psychologist, and his theory on cultural dimensions. This theory highlights the national differences between two cultures. Secondly, Richard R. Gesteland's theory on cross-cultural business behaviour will be addressed in this chapter. As the title of the theory indicates, it addresses a more business oriented view on cultural barriers than the theory of Geert Hofstede.

The construction of this chapter will be based and structured on Geert Hofstede's theory about the five cultural dimensions. The reason is that the five dimensions allow a clear structure in the chapter and makes it easier for the reader to understand it properly.

Geert Hofstede is often considered the creator and father of the theory about cultural national differences. His study on national differences includes the dimensions of *power distance, collectivism versus individualism, masculinity versus femininity, uncertainty avoidance* and *long-term versus short-term orientation* (Hofstede and Hofstede, 2005, p. 23 ff.). These dimensions are the general differences influencing the interaction between Danish and Indian individuals.

Secondly, the national differences identified in the analysis of Geert Hofstede's dimensions are in some sections further elaborated through Richard R. Gesteland's study on cross-cultural business cooperation. This theory deals with the following dimensions: *formal versus informal structures, direct versus indirect communication, monochronic versus polychronic time orientation, deal- versus relationship-focused cultures* and *reserved versus expressive communication* (Gesteland, 2005, pp. 17-19).

As mentioned the two theorist address culture from different perspectives, national- and business culture, and thereby complement each other. This gives a fundamental frame of cultural understanding and provides Danish companies with an adequate knowledge of cultural differences between Denmark and India.

The dimensions of the two above mentioned theories will not be further elaborated in this literature review, but in each section of the analysis based on Geert Hofstede's dimensions.

Power distance

Research question: How do Indian employees react with regard to formal hierarchy structure within the company?

To answer this question it would be beneficial to capture the essence of Hofstede's degree of power distance as a theoretical background. In every country, you will encounter some sort of inequality (Hofstede and Hofstede, 2005, p. 40). Hofstede points out that in every society you will find someone, who is wealthier, stronger and bigger (Hofstede and Hofstede, 2005 p. 40). In the light of this statement, Hofstede in his early studies (Hofstede, 1983) made a power distance index for many of the countries. Hofstede and Hofstede define power distance as:

"The extent to which the less powerful members of institutions and organisations within a country expect and accept that power is distributed unequally" (Hofstede and Hofstede, 2005, p. 46)

With this quotation and the basic understanding of power distance, how does it then occur in societies? Hofstede makes an explicit polarisation within the power distance. He talks about countries with a high power distance and countries with a low power distance. What is important, in this chapter, is how power distance is visible in a business context. In other words there is either a high or a low distance between leaders and subordinates within an organisation. Thereby not said, that power distance cannot be used in other contexts. Hofstede describes that the power distance is to be found in the family, the school, the business and the society (Hofstede and Hofstede, 2005, p. 51).

In countries, which score high on the power distance index, the organisation is highly hierarchically. In these countries there is a long distance between the manager and the subordinate concerning payment as well as daily interaction. The subordinate does not socialise with his superior and he is very dependent on his superior. The manager is expected to delegate tasks and the subordinate will do as told. In short, the subordinate and his superior are unequal.

The exactly opposite situation is the reality in countries scoring low on the power distance index. In these countries the manager and his/her subordinate are seen as equals. The subordinate will address the superior more lightly and work is done more independently. Rank is a matter of formalities or expertise and salary is more equally. The above mentioned differences are illustrated in Table 2.1.

Table 2.1: Key differences between low and high power distance

Low power distance	High power distance
• Flat organisations	• Pyramid structure
• Low hierarchy	• High hierarchy
• Equality between manager and subordinate	• Inequality between manager and subordinate
• Decentralisation is common	• Centralisation is common

Source: Own elaboration based on Hofstede and Hofstede (2005, p. 59)

Gesteland makes a similar distinction of culture within business. He talks about the formal versus the informal organisation (Gesteland, 2005, p. 47). Gesteland's work is fairly practical yet it seems to contribute to Hofstede's work with these counterparts concerning the formal and the informal culture. The informal culture is like the low scoring power distance cultures: *"... informal cultures value egalitarian attitudes with smaller differences in status and power"* (Gesteland, 2005, p. 47) and the formal cultures have similarities with the high scoring power distance cultures as: *"Formal cultures tend to be organised in hierarchies reflecting major differences in status and power"* (Gesteland, 2005, p. 47).

Gesteland lines up several examples of cultural clashes that might occur, when one is not familiar with these differences regarding formality. Furthermore, he points out that when dealing with very formal countries one might encounter some status-barriers if doing business with either a woman, a young person or one having a low rank in their own organisation (Gesteland, 2005, p. 53). Gesteland's distinctions are illustrated in Table 2.2.

Table 2.2: Key differences between informal and formal structures

Informal cultures	Formal cultures
• Minor differences in status and power	• Major differences in status and power
• Egalitarian attitude	• Non egalitarian attitude

Source: Own elaboration based on Gesteland (2005, p. 47)

Gesteland places India in the more formal end of the continuum (Gesteland, 2005, p. 129). He mentions that respect is rather important for the Indian people and particularly when it comes to respecting the elder. Moreover, the Hindu caste system also makes the Indian culture rather hierarchic (Gesteland, 2005, p. 130). Hofstede agrees with Gesteland's findings by giving India a score of 77 in the power distance index (Hofstede and Hofstede, 2005, pp. 43-44). As a comparison, Denmark scores 18 on the power distance index.

No doubt that there is a theoretical difference between Denmark and India concerning status, power and hierarchy. This leads to the question, whether or not the field trip to India will expose the same differences. The research indicates a difference in power distance, but also many similarities. Hofstede refers to India as one. This is a nation-wide distinction which in the learnings of the field trip is not enough. A more two-fold approach seems appropriate.

First of all, a general recognition of the high power distance is found in India. Several times the study group observed how the tone is very formal and how lower ranked people were much dependent on their superiors. Though the field trip intended to explore the culture of rather big companies, one would indeed learn a lot about culture just living the daily life in India. Further examples were found in the spare time of the field trip. In shops and restaurants the manager would constantly stand behind the employees, doing nothing but command the tasks. Even though this is a rather practical example, the group experienced this frequently, and it gives a good insight to the distance of power.

The company visits also revealed some connections to the high power distance. For instance three of the visits were made to domestic companies. The power, status and hierarchy were indeed visible here, where blue collar workers had less to say than white collar workers. Even though all companies had a "kaizen"-box**Fejl! Bogmærke er ikke defineret.**, the manager from one of the domestic companies, company Z, stated that the employees of course could suggest improvements, but they did not have the same organisational knowledge as the managers. In contrast to this, the manager of one of the global companies, company E, expressed that when Danes want to suggest something, they just address the right employee without considering their rank. In India minor suggestions can be addressed straight upward to the manager, but if it is a matter of major importance, a commission would be settled or it would go through the spokesperson.

Another clear aspect of the high power distance was seen in relation to the busses which some of the global companies, company C, D and F, have for their employees. Here the employees were divided in two groups; one of white collar workers and one of blue collar workers. The hierarchy was strong and the two groups were not mixed. This was also seen during lunch, where the employees of the different collar groups did not interact. Company C later changed this condition in an attempt to end the division in busses. This shows that the global companies especially differentiate on formalities regarding the power structure. Employees seem to have more influence in these companies, and if a problem occurs or an employee has a great idea for improvement, he or she is encouraged to speak up. Roughly speaking, the global companies seem to have a lower power distance. Even though people seem to be much more encouraged to interact between ranks and departments, the global companies still have some challenges regarding the integration and interaction between the collar groups along with other challenges that will be further elaborated below.

The Indians need clear descriptions of their assignments for instance regarding expectations, costs and time perspectives. This was indicated by company C and F. However, the main benefit of the Indian employees are that when the path is clear and the expectations are set, you get what you ask for and the quality is high. The reason for this is that in high power distance countries, people are more dependent on their superiors (Hofstede and Hofstede, 2005, p. 46). As an example, the global company E referred to an incident concerning an Indian employee visiting Denmark. He was in Denmark for educational reasons and to learn about the Danish working culture. He was expected to solve some tasks, but nothing happened, because his Danish superior did not describe the tasks in detail. At the end of the stay, both the superior and the employee were frustrated. This illustrates that in Denmark people are used to being more independent and that in India people are much more dependent on their superiors and need to have guidelines.

Finally, the Indians find it difficult to give feedback to their subordinates. Even though in the global companies the employees are allowed and encouraged to address their manager, they still have problems doing so. In fact, company C and E educate their employees in the art of giving a proper feedback to their superior. The challenges mentioned above demonstrate that not only do companies need to distinguish between the power distances, but they also need to take into account the underlying national values. This gives a deeper insight to the power distance in India, and why it is a rather difficult task to change the pattern for the global companies. Even though they might want a more Western oriented culture or a lower hiearchy, they have to understand that there is a tight cultural chain connected to the power distance starting with the roots of the family.

The results of this section enlighten how Indian employees react regarding hierarchies within a company. The results show that India is a country with a high power distance and a very formal culture. The field trip further exposes some variation to this. A much more flat structure is beginning to dominate the companies, but it is not without cultural challenges due to the underlying national culture.

Collectivism versus individualism

Research question: *To which degree is the Indian society collectivistic or individualistic?*

The following section will include an introduction to Hofstede's theory regarding national culture, specifically the dimension concerning collectivism versus individualism as well as Gesteland's theory concerning cross cultural business behaviour, specifically the dimensions, deal-focus versus relationship-focus and emotionally expressive versus emotionally reserved cultures. These theories are used in relation to answering the above mentioned research question.

Hofstede's dimension on collectivism versus individualism explains how societies vary between those in which individual needs are prioritised and those in which collectivistic needs are prioritised (Hofstede, 2001, p. 209). In the book, "*Culture's consequences*" from 1984 Hofstede states that the dimension individualism versus collectivism concerns the way in which people in a society live together. Hofstede states that in some cultures individualism is seen as a blessing and a source of well-being, whereas in other cultures collectivism and the well-being of the group is considered most important and individualism is seen as a sort of alienation from the society (Hofstede, 1984, p. 148). Hofstede further states that the relationship between the individual and the collectivism in a society is not only a matter of ways of living, but is directly linked to the social norms and values (Hofstede, 1984, p. 149). Therefore, issues concerning collectivism versus individualism are considered central issues to address and take into account when engaging in business cooperation between two different cultures.

In relation to the Indian culture the research of the field trip indicates that family values are considered very important in the Indian culture. This is illustrated by a global company, company D, which states that when Indians go out they return home around ten o'clock in the evening in order to spend time with their families. This statement is supported by another statement the global company E, explaining that the Indian culture contains a unique strong social system and family values. When you get married in India, the bride will move in with the parents of the groom. These statements indicate that collectivism and the well-being of the group in the

Indian culture is an important dimension. The field trip further indicated that the Indian culture is based on the belief that decisions should be made collectivistic and that the success rate is higher when working in groups rather than individually. Indians are able to make decisions and work on their own, whereas the Danish culture according to Hofstede is based more on an individualistic focus. Hofstede states that India possesses an individualism index of 48, whereas Denmark possesses an individualism index of 74 (Hofstede, 1984, p. 158). The level of the individualism index indicates that the Indian culture is focused on the view that individual initiative is socially frowned upon. Moreover, group decisions are considered to be better than individual decisions, and training and use of skills in jobs are considered important. The Danish culture is based on the view that individual initiatives are socially encouraged, individual decisions are considered better than group decisions and freedom and challenges are considered important factors in relation to jobs (Hofstede, 1984, p. 166).

The differences between the collectivistic culture, here seen as the Indian culture, versus the individualistic culture, here seen as the Danish culture, is further outlined by Hofstede. He states that some of the major differences between the two dimensions are that children in collectivistic cultures learn to think in terms of "we" whereas children in individualistic cultures learn to think in terms of "I". Furthermore, the relationship between employer and employee in collectivistic cultures is based on moral terms and a family link, whereas the relationship between employer and employee in an individualistic culture is based on a contract and a mutual advantage (Hofstede, 1994, p. 67).

The research indicated that when an Indian company hires new employees, they are "employed for life", this was stated by company A, which is consistent with Hofstede's analysis. Unions are big in India and therefore firing an employee is both frowned upon and for the employee seen as a mayor defeat. At the same time the research indicates that Indian employees are not always loyal towards their employers. Several of the global companies, company C, D, E and F, state that when presented to a wage increase, the Indian employees tend to leave the company. The research from the field trip indicated that although Indians often consider their work and colleagues like a family, many Indians tend to change job, when they are presented to something better. This often happens when Danish companies improve the Indian employee's skills through education and courses. Very often this has been dealt with and avoided trough a binding contract, stating that an employee, who is given educational training, has to stay with the company throughout a period of six months before he or she may leave the company. Another example shows that one of the domestic companies, company X, addresses problems happening in the production with a free line of communication. This means that all employees gather to discuss the issue and its origin to find a proper solution. This statement is further supported by a statement from the global company B that explains that the harmony in groups is crucial. If there is no harmony, no work will be done in the company. These statements further support the assumption, that the Indian culture is based on collectivism and that group decisions are considered more effective than individual decisions. The above mentioned characteristics of Hofstede's dimensions on individualism and collectivism are outlined in Table 2.3 below.

Table 2.3: Key difference between individualism and collectivism

Individualism	Collectivism
• Employees act in self interest • Fragmented point of view • People speak out their mind • Avoid hiring family members • Speak in terms of "I"	• Employees act in interest of the group • Holistic point of view • Direct confrontation should be avoided in order to keep harmony • Hire family members if possible • Speak in terms of "we"

Source: Own elaboration based on Hofstede (1994, p. 67)

While Hofstede's theory relates to the national culture of a country, Gesteland has specified his theory to relate only to business culture. One of the topics that Gesteland's theory concerns is the question of whether a culture is deal-focused or relationship-focused. Deal-focused people are task-oriented whereas a relationship focused society is people-oriented. A major difference between cultures that are deal-focused or relationship-focused is that developing rapport[1] is essential before talking business in relationship-focused societies. Conflicts often occur when two participants, one from a deal-focused and one from a relationship-focused culture respectively, try to engage in business. The conflict often occurs when deal-focused cultures do not take into account the importance of rapport before dealing with business. The relationship-focused individuals are then left with the impression that the deal-focused individual is offensive, pushy and dishonest (Gesteland, 2005, p. 18).

---

[1] Rapport is defined as a mutual relationship of trust between two parties. Furthermore also as taking the second position and be willing to try to understand and see the other parties' point of view (O'Conner, 2002, pp. 50-51).

According to the study of Gesteland, the Indian business culture is strongly relationship-focused and doing business in India is first of all related to getting to know your counterparts before getting into the business negotiations. Although Gesteland describes Indian culture to be strongly relationship-focused, he also explains that the new generation of business people in India tend to be more deal-focused, which indicates a change in the way of doing business in India from a relationship-focused to a more deal-focused orientation (Gesteland, 2005, p. 130).

Gesteland's research has shown that Danish business people will ask directly to the business related subjects, while Indian business people will start the conversation with a polite small talk before getting into the business related subjects. The domestic company Y explains that it is not possible for an Indian company to work with someone whom it does not trust. Others support this statement by explaining, that when working with Indian companies it is essential to be honest and not have a hidden agenda. The global company A states in India that business relations are often based on trust and that companies often engage in long term partnerships; when the partnership does no longer make sense, the companies part ways as friends.

Gesteland's analysis and the research from the field trip indicates that in the Danish deal-focused culture companies get to know their counterparts when talking business, unlike the Indian relationship-focused culture in which companies get to know their counterparts and establish rapport before talking business. The above mentioned is summarised in Table 2.4 below.

Table 2.4: Key differences between relationship-focus and deal-focus

Relationship-focus	Deal-focus
• Small talk is essential	• Small talk is less essential
• Takes weeks or months to learn about your counter partner	• Takes few days to learn about your counter partner
• Socialise before business	• Business right away

Source: Own elaboration based on Gesteland (2005, p. 21 ff.)

Another of Gesteland's dimensions, which is relevant to take into account when researching the Indian culture in regard to collectivism and individualism, is the dimension of emotionally expressive versus emotionally reserved cultures, when it comes to communication. The differences in the way of communicating between the two dimensions can result in a communication gap (Gesteland, 2005, p. 19). According to Gesteland's studies, the Indian communication culture is relatively reserved, which is also the case in Danish communication culture. Gesteland's study shows that the Danish modesty is a national characteristic (Gesteland, 2005, p. 292) and that the Indian people often tell you what you want to hear in an attempt to be polite instead of what you need to hear (Gesteland, 2005, p. 130). The research from the field trip reveals that Indians tend not to want to disappoint people, and therefore they tell you what you want to hear instead of what you need to hear. This is a result of the importance of relationships and the wish to keep a good relationship with one's partners, counterparts and so forth. Table 2.5 presents the key differences of this dimension.

Table 2.5: Key differences between emotionally expressive vs. emotionally reserved cultures

Emotionally expressive	Emotionally reserved
• Overlapping each other when communicating • Tell what the recipients need to hear instead of what they want to hear • Gesticulating	• Taking turns when communicating • Tell what the recipients want to hear instead of what they need to hear • Reserved

Source: Own elaboration based on Gesteland (2005, p. 69 ff.)

Summarised, the analysis of this research question has shown that the Danish and the Indian cultures are very different in relation to the way of conducting business and dealing with business partners. Where the Danish business culture is focused on getting to business as fast as possible, the Indian business culture is influenced by the importance of relationships and rapport between two parties. The analysis further indicates a different view on the strength concerning group work and decisions. Finally the analysis showed that both the Danes and the Indians are relatively emotionally reserved with regard to communication.

Uncertainty avoidance

Research question: *In what way does the Indian society control uncertainty regarding the future?*

Like the other dimensions mentioned above, this section will begin with an introduction to Hofstede's concept of uncertainty avoidance, which is borrowed from Cyert and March (Hofstede, 2001, p. 145). Uncertainty avoidance can be measured by a whole range of dimensions. However, this chapter is restricted to the dimensions regarding the uncertainty in the society and within business. As Hofstede writes, time has only one direction and we must accept a future that moves very fast, thereby we are living with an uncertainty of which we are conscious (Hofstede, 2001, p. 146). It varies from culture to culture how it adapts to uncertainty, and ways of coping with uncertainty belong to the cultural heritage of the society.

In order to deal with uncertainty organisations use technology, social rituals and rules. Technology refers to the use of computers, and social rituals in organisations include business meetings which have their own language and taboos. Uncertainty-avoiding rituals include writing memos, completing reports, accounting, planning and control systems. Rules are concerned with the way in which organisations try to reduce the internal uncertainty caused by the unpredictability of their members' and stakeholders' behaviour. It is important to note that the authority of rules is different from the authority of people. The first refers to uncertainty avoidance and the second to power distance (Hofstede, 2001, pp. 147-148). According to the above mentioned theory uncertainty avoidance can be defined as:

"The extent to which the members of a culture feel threatened by uncertain or unknown situations" (Hofstede, 1994, p. 113)

This can be expressed through nervous stress and a need for predictability, which is a request for written and unwritten rules. In countries that have a high uncertainty avoidance people come across quite busy, emotionally, actively and aggressively (Hofstede, 1983, p. 61). Furthermore, individuals do not like the unexpected, which demands a great need for rules and regulations to control the society and thereby avoid uncertain situations. Company rules should not be broken and there is a resistance toward change and only known risks are worth taking (Hofstede, 2001, pp. 160-161). In countries that have low uncertainty avoidance, people are controlled, lazy, easy-going and quiet and time is free (Hofstede, 1983, p. 61). Furthermore, there is an openness to change, new ideas and individuals do not fear unknown situations and are comfortable with experiments and challenges, which are considered stimulating and positive (Hofstede, 2001: 160-161). However it is important to note that these statements will vary depending on the emotional level of the observer (Hofstede, 1994, p. 115). In the following Table 2.6 the differences between high and low uncertainty avoidance are illustrated.

In order to distinguish between Denmark and India it is important to compare the uncertainty dimension of both nations. According to Hofstede, Denmark has a score of 23, whereas India has a score of 40 (Hofstede, 1983, p. 52). By comparing these scores, they both fall into the grouping of medium to low uncertainty avoidance (Hofstede, 1994, pp. 113-114).

In comparison to the other dimensions based on Hofstede's studies uncertainty avoidance is the one where the Danish and Indian culture is most alike. This makes the dimension the one with the greatest potential to successful corporation, compared to the other dimensions in Hofstede's studies. On the basis of these scores it is interesting to find out if these theoretical findings are also seen during the field trip.

Table 2.6: Key differences between low and high uncertainty avoidance

Low uncertainty avoidance	High uncertainty avoidance
<ul><li>Low resistance to change</li><li>Low stress and anxiety</li><li>People are lazy and quiet</li><li>Variation is curious</li></ul>	<ul><li>High resistance to change</li><li>High stress and anxiety</li><li>People come across busy, emotionally and actively</li><li>Variation is dangerous</li></ul>

Source: Own elaboration based on Hofstede (2001, p. 160)

As mentioned in the section on power distance, Hofstede generalises India to be only one culture, which is not enough; a two-fold approach seems more appropriate. It seems that there is a different approach to the uncertainty avoidance depending on whether you are in a domestic or global company. The following section will clarify this.

In relation to the domestic companies the dimension of uncertainty avoidance is not consistent with the findings from the analysis of Hofstede. It is important for these companies to plan the future, which is why they use control systems and investments with experts, as stated by company Y. Furthermore, company X states that many of the employees have worked in the company for many years. The domestic companies X and Y make short term and long term strategies based on the fact that they cannot afford to have only one strategy. The domestic companies Y and Z also state that a lot of time is spent on constructing contracts and it is very important to obey the standard operating procedures. These findings are characteristics for the dimension of high uncertainty avoidance (Hofstede, 2001, p. 160).

In the global companies there is another focus on the uncertainty avoidance which to a larger extent fits the findings of the studies of Hofstede. For instance, the global company D explains that it does not have a common approach to change. It needs to be prepared for and willing to make a change, because without change it will not survive. Company F states that mistakes will happen and this should also be accepted. Hofstede characterises low uncertainty avoidance as openness to change and curiosity towards differences (Hofstede, 2001, p. 160). This fits very well with the findings from the global companies.

There are some common traits in the domestic and global companies, company A, F and X, as these state that companies do not fire employees; typically they are hired for lifetime and agreed through contracts. This indicates high uncertainty avoidance (Hofstede, 2001, p. 161). Furthermore, the employees do not feel comfortable by expressing a problem, claim or anger. This is stated by the companies A and Y. This however is the opposite direction of low uncertainty avoidance (Hofstede, 2001, p. 161).

This section has acknowledged the fact that the dimension of uncertainty is not as transparent as the other of Hofstede's dimensions. The results of the analysis lead to the conclusion that it is extremely important for companies that decide to do business in India to be aware of these cultural differences. The field trip illustrates that the dimension is not a definitive solution. To answer the research question it can be concluded that the degree to which Indians control uncertainty regarding the future, depends on the contexts.

Masculinity versus femininity

Research question: *Which values define the Indian society?*

According to Hofstede, this question can be answered through his dimension on masculinity versus femininity. The dimension indicates the relative importance of job status, job security, cooperation, advancement and challenge, which relates to gender roles in society. Hofstede points out that there is a clear difference between how men and women interact in the same job. He states that men *"are socialised toward assertiveness and self-reliance,"* while women are socialised *"toward nurturance and responsibility"* (Hofstede, 1983, p. 55).

According to Hofstede's index, Denmark scores 16 and India scores 56 (Hofstede and Hofstede, 2006, p. 137). This indicates that India is a male-dominated country whereas Denmark is a female-dominated country. The gap between men and women values is much wider in India than in Denmark. Furthermore, it is a general assumption that women have no power in business context, which is why many jobs in senior management are occupied by men. This theoretical perspective is confirmed but also denied by the participating companies of the field trip.

In male-dominated societies the individuals are motivated by material success, career and power. Here are clearly defined gender roles according to which women are "soft" and expected to deal with emotions, while men are "hard" and expected to deal with the facts. In female-dominated societies, these gender-segregated boundaries are dissolved, which means that women and men are more similar and have equal opportunity to work with both emotion and facts (Hofstede and Hofstede, 2006, p. 135). The above mentioned is summarised in Table 2.7.

Table 2.7: Key differences in terms of masculinity and femininity

Masculinity	Femininity
• Work is a tool to obtain rewards, challenges and improvement in career	• Work is a tool to obtain better life quality; to nurse personal relationships
• Discrimination of women is a big issue	• Discrimination of women is a minor issue
• Higher job stress	• Lower job stress
• One's choice of job is determined by intrinsic interest	• One's choice of job is determined by career and status
• Only men work, women stay at home	• Both men and women work

Source: Own elaboration based on Hofstede and Hofstede (2005, pp. 115-162)

As already mentioned, status is important in a male-dominated society, which indicates pursuit of being the best and having a winning mentality (Hofstede, 1984, p. 63). Job recognition and status are both important for Indians, exemplified through the fact that companies do not easily fire their employees, as it is very hard for the employees' ego. Instead of firing employees, the companies tend to withhold new assignments, causing employees to search for new job opportunities elsewhere. This was stated by company B and confirmed by company C, adding that titles are very important for the Indians. One of the global companies, company D, stated that titles are so important for their employees that they invent new ones. In addition to this, the global company E points out that the Indian society works a lot more than eight hours a day. Thereby the employees prove that they can deliver and perform. This supports Hofstede`s assumption that one of the values for Indian society is performance (De Mooij and Hofstede, 2010, p. 89).

Hofstede's studies indicate that men are more outcome-driven in the business world than women (Hofstede, 1994, pp. 3-4). The global and domestic companies of this research partially agree with this theoretical statement. All the company managers are convinced that women have the same opportunities for success and authority as men. In continuation of this the global companies indicate that women are more motivated than men. Therefore, companies begin to employ more women and apply a policy, that the workforce shall contain a minimum percentage of women. This was stated by company B and F. Despite of this development the research shows a disharmony between what the organisation's managers present and what the employees explain. The employees explain that woman do not have the same authority as men, and that about 60 percent of the men are bound to have a problem with a female manager, which was stated by company C, E, and F. This is also the reason why companies sometimes hire an elderly man to gain or establish authority, which was indicated by company E. These findings comply with the masculine dimension.

As mentioned in the section about power distance, the hierarchical structure in India is high. This is supported by some of the global companies, C, D and F, and indicates that high authority is a part of the Indian culture, but the degree depends on the manager. This indicates that the feminine values slowly gain entrance. However, another global company, company E, explains that its organisational structure is high, but this is due to the fact that Indian society in general is used to have a masculine oriented manager. A general assumption is that Indians need little appreciation for a better working effort, which can be interpreted as an example that the Indian society contains a feminine dimension (Hofstede, 1994, pp. 3-4). Moreover, the domestic companies Y and Z believe in a more flat organisation, because it is time saving, and thereby they support the assumption about the Indian society containing a feminine dimension. Many of the companies, company C, D and F, focus on fringe benefits as for instance bus transportation to and from work. The domestic companies, company X, Y and Z, indicate that trust is a very important value in the Indian society. According to Hofstede, the term trust can be placed in the feminine dimension, as this is considered a soft value (Hofstede and Hofstede, 2006, p. 134). Naturally, trust is a valuable aspect of the Indian society compared to the collectivistic findings. The importance of the collectivistic society and the establishment of relationship cannot occur without trust. This again, indicates that even though the Indian society, according to Hofstede, is dominated by the masculine dimension, there are some values that refer to the feminine dimension. The above indicates that the feminine dimension gains ground in the values of Indian society.

To summarise, the values of the Indian society are mainly dominated by the masculine dimension, meaning that status is a very important aspect. The society is clearly divided concerning gender roles. The companies are mostly driven by male employees although a change seems to occur. Females are slowly gaining ground in the business world. Therefore some of the Indian society's values reflect the feminine dimension such as trust and caring.

Long term versus short term orientation

Research question: To which degree does time matter in the Indian culture?

The original theory on national culture from Hofstede did not contain a dimension on *time*. The theory was only concerned with the four previous examined dimensions on which country cultures differ. The fifth dimension of Hofstede's theory was thereby added to the original four dimensions (Hofstede and Hofstede, 2005, pp. 29-31). This dimension considers the long term and short term orientation and was found to be of significant interest when considering cooperation between two contradictory cultures.

It is possible to distinguish between cultures with long term orientation and cultures with short term orientation as they have a difference in value. As for the other four dimensions, Hofstede has made an index for several countries and regions. The index gives India a score of 61, making it a long term oriented country, whereas Denmark was given a score of 46 making it a shorter termed oriented country (Hofstede and Hofstede, 2005, p. 211). Hofstede and Hofstede (2005) define the distinction between long term orientation and short term orientation as follows:

"Long-term orientation (LTO) stands for the fostering of virtues oriented toward future rewards – in particular, perseverance and thrifts. Its opposite pole, short-term orientation, stands for the fostering of virtues related to the past and present – in particular, respect for tradition, preservation of "face", and fulfilling social obligations" (Hofstede and Hofstede, 2005, p. 210).

These definitions very adequately distinguish the two conflicting poles. Long term orientation is described as having a focus on the future together with a property of persistence and thrift. Persistence can be seen as the main key for pursuing a goal and as essential for having a successful business. Furthermore, the thrift in long term oriented societies, as India, leads to savings and capital which can be used for reinvestments by the individual employee and his or her family. In addition, long term oriented countries seem to have a belief in hierarchy together with a penetrating value of shame, which is highly associated with keeping one's commitments. The opposite pole, short term orientation, is described by Hofstede as having a focus on the past and the present, which leads to a strong belief in traditions, preserving one's face and pleasing the obligations of the society. Societies with short term orientation must, however, keep in mind that a redundant respect for traditions inhibit innovation and thereby the competiveness on the global market. Moreover, the propensity of protecting face can detract one from getting on with the business at hand (Hofstede and Hofstede, 2005, p. 218). Table 2.8 summarises the distinctions from Hofstede.

Table 2.8: Key differences between long-term and short-term orientation

Long-term orientation	Short-term orientation
• The focus is on long term market position • Perseverance and slower results • Money is saved for investments • You look further into the future • Steadiness and stability • You have a sense of shame	• The focus is on the bottom line • Quick results • Less money is saved for investments • You look at the near future • Adaptability • You are concerned with "face"

Source: Own elaboration based on Hofstede (1994, p. 225)

The field trip showed very clearly that Indians look differently at time than the study group from Denmark. It was obvious that in India time is not linear and not at all as important as it is in western societies. An observation was made on this aspect. Several times the study group, due to the traffic, arrived either too early or a bit late for the arranged meetings. In Denmark you are expected to show up at the scheduled time – not ten minutes early or late. This fact meant that the research group was very uncomfortable, when arriving too early or too late for the meetings. In fact, in the cases of being too early it was discussed if the group should wait outside. The study group decided not to, which turned out to be the right decision in the context. The companies were always ready to welcome the group. Company A and C made it clear that this was normal, as the infrastructure makes it almost impossible to reach a place in time. In Hofstede's studies on long term oriented countries he also found the aspect of punctuality to be different from short term oriented countries. Societies with long term orientation typically forgive a lack of punctuality and do not mind a changing game-plan as an impact of a changing reality (Hofstede and Hofstede, 2005, p. 207 ff.).

The field trip also found indications on the long term orientation, which is the fact for India. Every organisation which was visited during the field trip, regardless of it being a domestic or global company, either directly said that short term relationships did not work, or indirectly indicated it by implying that long term relationships is the most appropriate way of doing business. This is consistent with the long term oriented way of thinking. The main focus is not this year's profit, but more importantly the profit ten years from now. These findings indicate that there is a possible conflict in relation to the cooperation between a long term and short term oriented country.

The short term oriented country will focus very much on the results now and here and has a specific focus on each year's profit. Furthermore, it is expected in a short term oriented country that deadlines are held and that punctuality is respected. Time is furthermore, according to the Indian employees, given a more human value, which means that you cannot control it completely. This was stated by company E. Contracting between two countries with differences in long- and short term orientation is therefore difficult as the values and things you appreciate are conflicting. A balance of expectations with your Indian counterparts is therefore crucial for successful business.

Gesteland and Gesteland (2010) distinguish between polychronic and monochronic time behaviour. Polychronic time cultures, such as India, typically have a lack of punctuality, allow frequent interruptions and multitasking during meetings, as well as late deliveries and missed deadlines are characteristics of this time behaviour (Gesteland and Gesteland, 2010, p. 29). This value of time perception typically bothers monochronic visitors and expatriates who have a contrasting way of perceiving time. In monochronic time cultures, such as Denmark, punctuality is strictly expected. Meetings start on time and proceed without interruptions as well as business people focus on doing one thing at a time. Furthermore, in contrast to the polychronic time behaviour, deadlines and delivery dates are sacred (Gesteland and Gesteland, 2010, p. 22). Gesteland's dimension on time is illustrated in Table 2.9.

Table 2.9: Key differences between polychronic and monochronic cultures

Monochronic	Polychronic
• Punctuality • Concrete schedules • Fixed agendas • Clock-obsessed	• Less punctual • Loose schedules • Agendas are more flexible • Time is less important

Source: Own elaboration based on Gesteland (2005, p. 59)

The field trip showed the difference between India's polychronic perception of time as a contrast to the monochronic sense of time that characterises the Western way of doing business. Several of the global companies indicate that they have trouble complying with the time frame of a task. 'By the end of the month' could easily mean 'by the end of the year', according to company C and E. This show very clearly that time is not a critical value in India as compared to Denmark where deadlines are very sacred and often a key to successful business. However, it is also important to recognise that India is changing and is slowly adopting a more Western mind-set as to the perception of time. The Indians begin to understand the rules of partnering with the West and many Indian employees are therefore very aware of the difference in time perception. They know that their Western partners have a more monochronic time behaviour. One of the global companies, company C, had a set of rules for meetings hanging on the wall, which reminded the Indian employees that it was not acceptable to be late for a meeting. This set of rules indicates an awareness of different time perception, and a possible solution as to how to handle it. Other examples of handling the difference in time behaviour were observed in some global companies, company C. D and E. Managers from these companies indicated that the Indian employees need a plan and deadline to handle the task in a reasonable frame of time. When having this frame, the Indians have become better at meeting the deadlines. Despite this improvement it is reasonable to take precautions, as their understanding of time is deeply rooted in their national culture. It can be difficult for a polychronic counterpart to enforce Indians to comply with rigid deadlines. Instead it can be useful to simply set a deadline earlier than needed. Furthermore, the polychronic counterpart , when deadline is coming closer, should stay in frequent touch with the monochronic counterparts to ensure progress.

To sum up, the field trip indicates a difference in time behaviour due to the national culture and a bad infrastructure. The study group got the clear impression that there was a much polarised perception of time.

However, the Indian employees are trying to adapt to the Western time perception in terms of business, as they are aware of the importance of this in the Western societies. The companies almost all indicate that they are adapting a more Western sense of business over time in order to stay competive and meet the demand as a supplier, customer and partner in the Western companies. Gesteland also seems to indicate that the behaviour of Indian suppliers, customers and partners slowly will come closer to the monochronic expectations (Gesteland and Gesteland, 2010, p. 29).

Implications

The implications summarised in Table 2.10 clearly indicate that the findings of the field trip do not completely agree with the general assumptions of the theoretical study by Hofstede. To address the disagreement between the findings and the general assumptions, the implications address the way in which Danish companies can handle and solve the cultural issues. An important notion is that the general assumptions are concerned with India in general. The field trip only covered the city of Chennai in the Tamil Nadu region. The companies clearly state that the difference between the Northern part of India and the Southern part of India is rather prominent. The only thing more difficult than to be indifferent to India would be to describe or understand India completely. Our findings and research are therefore not sufficient for companies planning to invest in business in the Northern part of India, nor are the general assumptions presented by former theorists. This field trip and book covers some of the implications you have to be aware of when you interact with an Indian culture in the Southern part of India.

A further important notation in this implication is awareness of the corruption in India. The companies included in this field trip, domestic as well as global, point at this to be a problem, but still a everyday issue. Some companies reject corruption, others state that if you know that your competitors engage in corruption, you must be aware of the advantages they gain from doing so.

Another challenge to take in mind is the strong family ties within the families. When Indian managers hire new employees, they might have a preference for family members or other close relatives, even though they are not the best candidate for the job. This can result in nepotism, and one of the global campanies actually had to let the manager go because of this.

Finally the section will outline the four funniest observations during the field trip:

- *How to Nod:* In India they do not nod the way Western people do. Instead of doing a back and forth nodding the Indians shake their head sideways.
- *The moustache:* Status is important in India. A way in which to demonstrate status is the men's moustache. The greater the moustache - the greater the status.
- *How to eat:* Always use your right hand to eat, regardless of using utensils or your fingers. The left hand is used for another purpose!
- *Be careful of your footwear:* It is very important to apologise immediately if one touches someone with his or her shoe or sandal.

Table 2.10: Implications of research questions

RQ 1 – How do Indian employees react in regard to formal hierarchy structure within the company?		
General assumption *High Power distance:* The Indian hierarchy is rather high and strict. There is a lot of inequality and employees are highly dependent on their supervisors.	**Findings** Even though this is the general assumption, this study found that the approach is more twofold. Many Indian companies are moving towards a more Western way of organising which indicates a lower power distance. Furthermore, the employees seem more independent in their work and rely less on their supervisors	**Implications:** The findings indicate that Danish companies should be aware of the high hierarchy. This means that Danish companies have to consider the dependency between the manager and the employee, and therefore clear tasks and direct commands need to be present. Furthermore Danish companies should consider educating their employees to get a better understanding of the corporation cultures.
RQ 2 - To which degree is the Indian society collectivistic or individualistic?		
General assumption *Collectivistic society:* The Indians very often think in terms of "we". They act in groups and friendship is predetermined by in-group. There are strong family ties and you are never alone. People live with or close to relatives.	**Findings** The findings indicate that the Indians primarily have a collectivistic orientation. They enjoy working in groups. However, this study found that some employees prefer to have individual work tasks and make their own decisions.	**Implications** The findings indicate that Danish companies should take into account the importance of rapport and dedicate time to build a relationship with their Indian counterparts. This could be done through social arrangements and calculate extra time for small talk in meetings. Furthermore Danish companies should consider the adjustments of work routines to ensure the Indian efficiency through collectivistic workflows.

RQ 3 - In what way does the Indian society control uncertainty regarding the future?		
General assumption	**Findings**	**Implications**
Medium to low uncertainty avoidance: This is the dimension on which Denmark and India are most similar, which makes it easier for Danish companies to interact with Indian companies.	The research indicates that the findings are not consistent with the general assumptions by Hofstede. This is based on the fact that it depends on whether the companies are global or domestic, as they react differently on uncertainty.	The findings indicate that Danish companies should be aware of the importance of control systems and the investments in experts in relation to cooperation with domestic companies. In relation to the establishment of an offshore department, the Danish companies must be willing to take risks and be adaptable to change.
RQ 4 - Which values define the Indian society?		
General assumption	**Findings**	**Implications**
Masculine society: The Indian society is fairly masculine. Women are expected to be tender and represent soft values, while men shall be tough and represent hard values. Status is very important. There is sympathy for stronger persons and a winning mentality.	Although the findings have shown that the Indian culture has changed in regard to women's role in society, women are still underrepresented in companies. Especially the global companies wish to have a fairer share of women in the working force. The masculine values are also shown in the way Indians strive towards status and improvements.	The findings indicate that Danish companies should be aware of the fact that about 60 % of all male employees have a problem regarding female leadership. Danish companies should therefore be aware of the possible conflicts in relation to using female leaders and the benefits of using male leaders. A solution for Danish companies can be to introduce a HR strategy with a minimum percentage of female employees. The introduction of a female employee should be done by an elderly male of high status, as he is respected by the current male employees. This results in respect for the new female employee. Furthermore, status is a high motivation factor in India and Danish companies can therefore benefit from implementing status incentives when cooperating with India.

RQ 5 - To what degree does time matter in the Indian society?		
General assumption	**Findings**	**Implications**
Long term orientation: The most important event in life will occur in the future. Persistence is seen as the main key for pursuing a goal. Within this dimension a culture is dependent on long term relationships which are highly associated with keeping ones commitments. Time is fluent.	The findings are consistent with the general assumptions. However, there is an indication that the Indian companies are adapting a more Western sense of business behaviour in terms of time perception. This has resulted in the fact that punctuality has improved.	The findings indicate that it can be difficult for Danish companies to enforce Indians to comply with rigid deadlines. To handle this problem it can be useful to simply set a deadline earlier than needed and at the time leading to a scheduled deadline, Danish companies should stay in frequent touch with the Indian counterparts to ensure progress.

Source: Own elaboration

Conclusion

This chapter addressed the issue of cultural differences between Denmark and India in a business perspective.

The *first research question* is concerned with the formal hierarchy within a company. The field trip conflicted with the theoretical statements of Hofstede and Gesteland. In Hofstede's studies he found power distance to be very high in the Indian society. This conflicts with the findings of this research, as the global companies in India turned out to be more Western oriented and thereby less hierarchical, whereas the domestic companies were more hierarchical and without Western influence. This distinction between global and domestic companies is missing in Hofstede's cultural dimensions. Gesteland's dimension on informal versus formal cultures yields the same constraints. Danish companies have to consider the dependency between the managers and the employees, and therefore clear tasks and direct commands need to be present. In order to get a better understanding of the cooperating cultures, cultural education would furthermore be beneficial for the Danish companies.

The *second research question* dealt with India as a collectivistic society in comparison with Denmark as an individualistic society. Equal to Hofstede's studies the research found that the Indian society values family and group relations higher than the individual needs. This makes relationships a very important issue in Indian business. In continuation of this, it was found that Indians focus on small talk before business, which is different from most Western societies, where business is approached directly without small talk.

This is in compliance with Gesteland's studies and theoretical framework, as he also points out that Indians are emotionally expressive. When doing business in India, rapport created through social arrangements and dedication of time for small talk is crucial for Danish companies. Without trust it is simply impossible to engage in successful business cooperation. Furthermore Danish companies should have in mind that teamwork and team decision-making is important in India, and is preferred instead of the individualistic approach in Danish culture.

The *third research question* focused on how the Indian society controls uncertainties regarding the future. Uncertainty avoidance is the dimension at which the Danish and Indian cultures are most alike. This reduces the dimension as a barrier in cooperating with India. The analysis has shown that the global companies to a larger extent fit with the findings from Hofstede, whereas a bigger deviation is found in the domestic companies. Therefore, Danish companies must be aware of the importance of control systems and the investments in experts in relation to cooperation with domestic companies. When establishing an offshore department, willingness to take risks and be adaptable to change is crucial for the Danish companies. The above-mentioned implications illustrate that the overall finding of uncertainty avoidance depends on the business context.

The *fourth research question* concerned the values that define the Indian society. Findings indicated that India is a masculine dominated country which agrees with Hofstede's studies on cultural dimensions. The field trip showed that even though the feminine dimension was slowly progressing in business, it is for example still an issue in some companies to have a woman in a leading position. Other key values found were status, power and economical improvements. The implications found that the Danish companies should consider introducing a HR strategy with a minimum percentage of female employees. The introduction of a female employee can beneficially be made by an elderly male of high status. Furthermore, Danish companies can benefit from implementing status incentives when cooperating with India.

The *final research question*, in which the time perception was in focus showed clear agreement with Hofstede and Gesteland's studies. In India time is fluent which means that punctuality is less present compared to Western societies. Though, it was found that the global companies were moving more towards a monochronic perception of time as they are aware of the importance of time for Western partners. To comply with the problem of rigid deadlines, Danish companies can set deadlines earlier than needed and stay in frequent touch with the Indian counterparts to ensure progress.

To conclude upon the research questions it is clear that India has moved towards a more global orientation. However, it is important when doing business with India to have the Indian culture in mind as they are very dedicated to their national culture, which influence their forms of business.

CHAPTER 3

Innovation in India

Maria Sudarschini Yogasundram, Tina Møller Jensen, Ena Cerimagic, Jesper Amstrup Hjelt & Louise Beck Jochumsen

Abstract

The content of this chapter is based on a field study including nine case companies in Chennai, India. The main drivers that international companies must cope with when innovating in India are outlined. The empirical findings of the field study seek to clarify in which areas international and Indian companies innovate and the three types of innovation in terms of product, process and paradigm are defined in relation to the case companies. Furthermore, the investigation indicates that process and product innovation are of main focus, potentially beneficial within knowledge hub industries, and through cooperation between equally internationalised companies.

Introduction

India is among the world's fastest growing emerging markets with annual growth rates of 6-8 percent (Udenrigsministeriet, 2011). The country has been able to evolve from a position of technology borrower to a role of technology innovator. It is a major destination of Foreign Direct Investment (FDI) in R&D and an attractive knowledge-based location for transnational corporations (European Commision, 2013). But how do Danish companies exploit the opportunities in terms of innovation and what are the key opportunities that differentiate India from other emerging economies? These questions will be addressed in this chapter, as relevant macroeconomic factors affecting innovation in India are introduced followed by a section analysing the case companies' use of innovation. This will result in an analysis of how Danish companies can utilise India and Indian companies in their innovation efforts.

Research questions

The purpose of this chapter is to determine how India works with innovation. This will be answered through the following three research questions.

1. *What are the current drivers of innovation in India?*
2. *In which areas do Danish and Indian companies innovate in India?*
3. *What other factors should Danish and Indian companies be aware of regarding innovation?*

Literature review

Innovation is increasingly seen as a powerful way of securing competitive advantage and a more secure approach to defending strategic positions (Tidd and Bessant, 2009, p. 17). The term 'innovation' is widely discussed and different authors have contributed to the definition. As the term 'innovation' has evolved over time, this section will review the most important developments in the literature. This discussion will help define the view on innovation used in this chapter and develop a framework from which the research questions will be answered.

One of the first to introduce the concept of 'innovation' was Joseph Schumpeter in "Capitalism, Socialism and Democracy" (1942). Schumpeter describes how innovation is the core of 'creative destruction'. Creative destruction is understood as the process that occurs, when businesses as part of a constant competition make yesterday's products obsolete by innovating and creating new and better products. According to Schumpeter (1942) it requires enterprises that are able to adapt to and take advantage of this process (1942, pp. 81-87). Innovation, according to Schumpeter (1934, p. 60), covers:

1. *The introduction of a new good or a new quality of the good*
2. *The introduction of a new method of production*
3. *The opening of a new market*
4. *The conquest of a new source of supply*
5. *The carrying out of the new organisation of an industry*

Brian S. Cumming (1998) gives an overview of several authors' definition of innovation developed in the period from 1968 to 1990. Cumming realises that the authors' definitions, as Schumpeter, focus on new products and new production process. However, Schumpeter also had other dimensions to his definition of innovation, such as the opening of a new market. The first author Cumming refers to is the Zukerman Committee which in 1968 defined innovation as *"a series of technical and commercial steps"* (Cumming, 1998, p. 21). Furthermore, Cumming refers to a literature study by Tinnesand from 1973. He studied 188 publications and found that the most dominant definition of innovation is *"the introduction of a new idea"* (Cumming, 1998, p. 21). Cumming also mentions the definition by DTI[2], who define innovation as *"the process of taking new ideas effectively and profitably through to satisfied customers"* (Cumming, 1998, p. 21).

Many other authors have their own definition of innovation. Abernathy and Clark (1985) defined it as the initial market introduction of a new product or process whose design departs radically from the past practice. Abernathy and Clark (1985) developed the *"transilience map"*, which shows the capacity of an innovation to influence the company's existing resources, skills and knowledge considering two distinct perspectives; the 'traditional' that focuses on how new technology and manufacturing activities are being organised and the second perspective that deals with the activities needed by the company to service new markets and customers.

Damanpour (1996) defines innovation as *"the adaption of an idea or behaviour new to the adopting organisations"* (Damanpour, 1996, p. 694). Similar to the other authors, Damanpour states that innovation covers a number of areas, including new products or services and new processes. Damanpour differs by including organisational structure as a new dimension (Damanpour, 1996).

As seen, many different approaches can be used in order for companies to explore opportunities for innovation. The above discussion leads to Table 3.1, which gives an overview of the areas of innovation covered by the reviewed authors.

Table 3.1: Overview of areas of innovation

Author / Innovative area	Process	Product	Market	Organizational structure
Schumpeter (1934)	X	X	X	
Tinnesand (1973)	X	X		
Robertson (1974)	X	X		
DTI (1996)	X	X		
Abernathy and Clark (1985)	X	X	X	
Damapour (1996)	X	X		X

Source: Own creation

---

[2] DTI is a department of the UK governmental Department for Business Enterprise and Regulatory.

Table 3.1 shows that none of the authors' definition covers all four areas of innovation. This leads to Tidd and Bessant who developed a model covering all four areas. The model contains four Ps, which can be used to explore opportunities for innovation; product, process, position or paradigm. Product is when a company is rethinking the design of the product and creates a new model, where process is about the way in which the new model would actually be built and concerns a new improved process of making this new model. Position involves rethinking the target market and paradigm is about 'how we frame what we do' and relates to innovation that defines or redefines the dominant paradigms of an organisation.

The process and product in Table 3.1 are equivalent to those of Tidd and Bessant (2009). Market can be seen as position and organisational structure as paradigm. The model makes it simple to identify innovation in the different areas. Furthermore it does not focus on a specific area in the field of innovation but allows for various forms of innovation. This chapter will therefore be based on this model and Tidd and Bessant's definition of innovation: *"…the process of turning opportunity into new ideas and putting these into widely used practice"* (Tidd and Bessant, 2009, p. 16).

The 4P framework contains four categories and innovation can happen within one or more of these:

- *Product innovation - changes in the (products/services) that the company offers.*
- *Process innovation – changes in the ways in which they are created and delivered.*
- *Position innovation - changes in the context in which the product/services are introduced.*
- *Paradigm innovation - changes in the underlying mental models which frame what the organisation does* (Tidd and Bessant, 2009, p. 21).

Tidd and Bessant (2009) also discuss the degree of novelty, running from minor incremental improvements to radical changes. Incremental change is the use and development of the already known, 'doing what we do better'. Radical change is search of new initiatives, where the company develops and creates new routines, 'doing something different' (Tidd and Bessant, 2009, p. 27). The 4Ps and the degree of innovation are illustrated in Figure 3.1.

Figure 3.1: The 4P model in relation to the degree of innovation

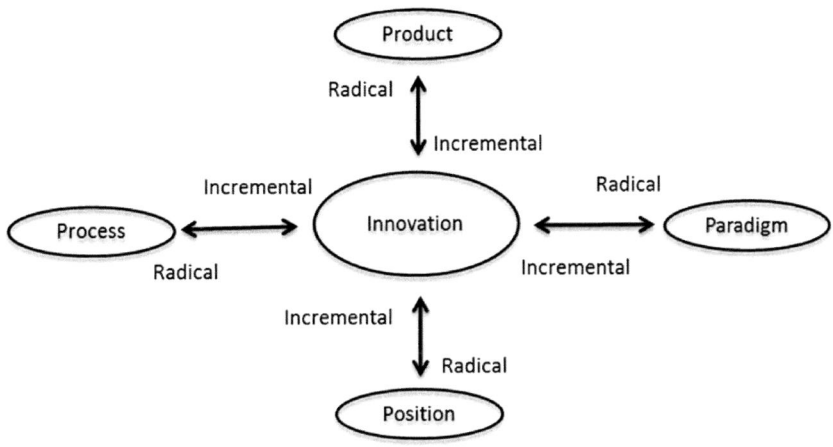

Source: Tidd and Bessant (2009)

Drivers for innovation

In relation to the 4Ps, factors that drive innovation are discussed. This section will therefore be based on De Wit and Meyer's (2010) model of *'Drivers of industry development'* containing four factors which drive innovation. De Wit and Meyer (2010) define what the different drivers may include:
"- Socio-cultural drivers can be changing health needs, environmental awareness and consumption habits
- Economical drivers can be changing exchange habits, economic growth and labour productivity.
- Political/regulatory can be drivers of new trade regulations, environmental laws and privatisation moves.
- Technological drivers can be new scientific breakthroughs, innovative technologies and communication standards" (De Wit and Meyer, 2010, p. 431).

De Wit and Meyer's model is used in this chapter as inspiration for the model shown in Figure 3.2. The four drivers are combined with the 4Ps to show how these elements affect and are affected by innovation. The focus will be on how these drivers influence innovation in India.

Figure 3.2: Interaction between main drivers and the 4Ps

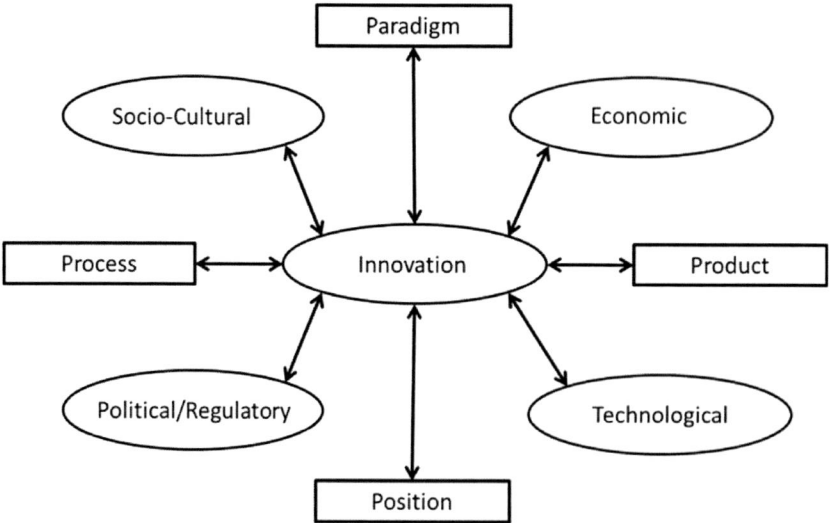

Source: Author's creation inspired by De Wit and Meyer (2010) and Tidd and Bessant (2009)

Figure 3.2 shows that the elements influence each other and the framework will help answer the research questions of this chapter. It shows how the elements affect the decision of how to integrate innovation when doing business in India. The model takes both macroeconomic and company-specific elements into consideration, giving an overview of the current possibilities and challenges.

Methodology

As preparation for the field study, a theoretical research was carried out to ensure a basic understanding of innovation, along with a study of scientific articles and literature to support empirical findings. Furthermore the theoretical research is undertaken to create a more concrete framework for the empirical data.

The desk and field research serves as the foundation for this chapter. The empirical data is collected through semi-structured interviews with nine different companies in Chennai, three Indian and six Danish companies. The companies represent a broad range of industries, which allows the analysis of innovation to take a broader perspective and define innovation across different industries.

The research questions were sent to the companies prior to the trip, offering the opportunity to prepare answers and a presentation. The interviewees are both of Danish and Indian nationality.

The main research drive was to explore how the case companies are working with innovation in India. As case studies have been conducted in several companies, a multiple case study approach is taken, which allows comparison of the different cases. A disadvantage of this approach is that the statements only represent the values and opinions of representatives, which affects the reliability and validity of the research. The purpose of the qualitative analysis is to give an objective guideline to companies that consider initiating innovation activities in India.

Drivers for innovation

The outset of this section will be the model *Drivers of industry development* (De Wit and Meyer, 2010, p. 431) in order to answer the first research question; *'What drives innovation in India?'*

The drivers will complement the 4Ps as an analysis at macro level. It will thus take into consideration the external factors that influence industry development in India.

Political/regulatory drivers

The political and regulatory drivers consist of drivers originating from governmental instances. The government can motivate companies to be more innovative through economic motivators, initiatives or by allowing better infrastructure, better possibilities for start-ups or more transparent legislation (De Wit and Meyer, 2010).

Realising that innovation will aid the growth of prosperity and national competitiveness, the President of India declared 2010-2020 the 'Decade of Innovation' (Innovation Council India, 2010). The statement is followed by establishing National Innovation Council (NInC), which focuses on five key parameters: platform, discourse, drivers, eco-system and inclusion. One initiative from the NInC is the India Innovation Portal, which provides a networking channel for innovators as well as support (Innovation Council India, 2010). Additionally, 'India Innovation Initiative' (I3) was launched in 2009 (The Hindu, 2009) to *"...support Innovation Ecosystem in the country by sensitising, encouraging and rewarding innovators and by facilitating commercialisation and start-up incubation of potential innovations"* (Department of Science and Technology). It is a nationwide competition for people above the age of 18 (Department of Science and Technology), recognising the growing young population of India (Dahlman and Utz, 2007, p. 129) as well as the need to create almost 15 million jobs every year (Department of Science and Technology).

The National Innovation Foundation was formed to support grassroots innovators financially and to specifically look at technical innovations in any field of human survival (National Innovation Foundation 2004-2013). By studying the different initiatives in depth, Danish companies can gain competitive advantage, as they will be able to receive funding, technical support and knowhow. Furthermore, the government is opening up to international companies, as new legislation allows different industries more ownership of their operations in India (Patel, et al. 2012). For example, single brand retailers can now own 100 percent of their Indian operations, compared to the 51 percent that has been the maximum since 2006 (Patel, et al., 2012). This can pose as a driver for Danish companies to invest more in R&D in India.

Finally, the fact that the Indian Government supports in-house R&D expenditures in India with 75-80 percent gives an incentive for international companies to place their R&D and innovations efforts physically in India. The incentives include a weighted tax deduction of 200 percent for companies engaged in manufacturing with in-house R&D, no import duty on import of capital goods for R&D and many more (Deloitte, 2011). The decision to move R&D and innovation efforts to India can be greatly influenced by these benefits. It is evident from this that the Indian Government seeks to promote and motivate innovation. Only a few identified factors are presented, which means the government is doing much more to foster innovation in India.

Despite the many initiatives promoting innovation, a highly fragmented market, corruption, bureaucracy and price sensitivity indicate that the Indian market is still an unsecure market for investments. The Indian market is closed through high tariff barriers, thus an agreement on free trade between EU and India would help to improve these issues (Udenrigsministeriet, 2011). These factors should also be studied thoroughly, when making a decision about investing in innovation in India.

Socio-cultural drivers

The socio-cultural drivers consist of the social and cultural developments that can motivate innovations. For example, a country's demographics can have an effect on the dominant level and type of innovations.

More than half of India's population is below the age of 25 (India Online Pages, 2013), serving as a driver in several ways. First, the growing young population can be educated towards being innovative and thereby serve as a driver themselves. Second, the large segment of young people will have needs that are different from those of an old population, posing as a market opportunity. Finally, it can change the culture itself, as it is plausible that a younger generation will break away from the caste system, or lower the meaning of it, which could change the hierarchy of people.

Green energy serves as a driver by opening up for new markets and new potential innovations such as solar and wind energy or other innovations that could revolutionise the sector (Patankar). Green innovation includes everything from new products, techniques and new policies which are all mainly used in order to meet the requirements of the Indian population and companies (India Online Pages, 2013). Based on observations done in India, the energy area is mainly regulatory driven, which is going to have an impact on the economic, environmental and the social factors for India's growth in the future. A new market can arise through green innovation where ideas help the poor part of the population, who are in need for basic things like clean drinking water (Kaul, 2013). The growing Indian population will inevitably demand better conditions of living at some point, building an opportunity in itself for innovation.

The educational system also plays a role for the Indian society by securing that Indian employees are skilled in foreign languages and business related subjects in order to make these employees attractive for international companies, company A. But there are limitations for the individual Indian wanting to access a higher education, as the cost of the study is too high or the specific education is not offered in the country or region (Perumal, 2013).

Technological drivers

Technological drivers primarily consist of product innovations themselves that in turn enable further innovation. They can also be developments in communication standards and/or technologies, which can ease the innovation processes or they can be breakthroughs in science that can foster new innovations (De Wit and Meyer, 2010).

India's innovation efforts benefit from developments in communication technology (Government of India, n.d.). Video Conferencing (VC), cell phones (and a supporting telecommunication network) and other developments in communication technology are all technologies that enable innovation, in the sense that they make real-time communication possible (Keeble, 2013).

The fact that cell phone ownership in the general public in India is increasing (TRAI, 2012) is a driver for innovation as well. Danish companies can develop communication systems that are specifically useful in India with the given conditions present, as for example poverty conditions or a large population of young people, as identified in socio-cultural drivers.

Technological innovations within as well as outside of India can pose as a driver for innovation as they can be subject for further development. An example of this is Gillette who experienced challenges when entering the Indian market.

Realising that a big part of the Indian men do not have access to running water, Gillette adapted the razor to fit these needs (AP Reporter, 2013). Similar adaptions in products or services that are already developed and marketed in other countries can be a driver for innovations in India.

A Danish company could take starting point in its core competencies, look into the specific needs in India and develop country specific alterations to existing products or services to fit the Indian market, or it can utilise country specific competencies in India to develop products for the international market. The incentives offered by the Indian Government, as mentioned before, are relevant to remember in this context.

In a report by the McKinsey Global Institute (Manyika et al., 2013), 12 potential disruptive technologies are identified. They are all known technologies, but still subject to further innovation. These technologies can be important for Danish companies working within these areas when considering increasing innovation efforts in India. Finally, Danish companies can further develop technologies related to inclusive innovation as identified under socio-cultural drivers.

As seen above, there are several opportunities for Danish companies to pursue with regards to technological drivers in India. Some are more specific to India than others, so it is important for the company to make sure that its core competencies and the benefits of placing R&D in India with a focus on the end market are aligned to create a competitive advantage.

Economic drivers

One key economic driver is the Indian government. As mentioned above, the Indian government financially supports companies trying to innovate

(Innovation Council India 2010). Another economic driver is the inflation, which has increased drastically lately and has led to an increase in food and diesel prices. The inflation shows that many of the goods produced in India increase by 2,03 percent each month making it harder for people to buy essential goods (Rajesh, 2013). In addition, more than 29,8 percent of the Indian population live for less than 56 cents a day and the increasing inflation makes it harder for this segment to survive. There is a market opportunity for innovative companies if they are able to find new ways of satisfying the basic need of a common Indian living below the poverty line (Dahlman and Utz, 2007).

Finally, an increasing population and almost 30 percent of the population living below the poverty line, requires a large amount of manufactured goods that should be exported in order for the GNP to have a positive effect on the Indian economy (Trading Economics, 2013). Indian economy have major challenges with growing population, poverty, unemployment and the fact that 70 percent of the Indian population still are living in countryside villages (Maps Of India, n.d.). In order for the economy to grow, these changes must be handled first (Maps Of India).

Part conclusion

The section above outlines external drivers which could influence innovation in India. A series of focus areas that could have great impact on the overall innovation have been suggested through the four drivers for innovation. It is important for companies doing innovation in India to take the drivers into consideration as they can pose as both opportunities and threats depending on how they are handled. For the political drivers, the government is a valuable partner in promoting innovation. It has developed different initiatives to strengthen this development. Furthermore the government has opened up for more ownership by foreign companies. However, much still remains in order to make India a more attractive business partner in innovation.

In terms of demography, the young population means that India possesses a strong workforce, which can enable innovation. However, to fully exploit this opportunity a reform in the educational system has to be made to ensure that the graduates will acquire the needed knowledge. Technological drivers mainly consist of product innovation which is vital for the country's competitive advantage and further development. Finally, the economical drivers identify high growth and inflation as relevant factors. High growth indicates that it is a booming economy with potential for further investments. Unfortunately, due to the high growth the country has also been experiencing a high inflation rate, which increases uncertainty for foreign investors. The high inflation also decreases the living conditions of the poor, as prices on food increase and makes it harder for this part of the population to make a living.

Analysis of the case companies

This section will turn the focus to the case companies in relation to the 4Ps and the level of innovation; incremental and radical. The 4Ps of innovation include process, position, paradigm and product. Position innovation is excluded due to lack of empirical findings in the case company investigation. The analysis will provide an overview of the areas in which the companies innovate in India, which will be a basis for a general understanding of innovation in India. The purpose of this section is to understand how a Danish company can cooperate with Indian companies when innovating. The analysis is primarily based on the field study. The Danish companies will be referred to as cases A, B, C, D, E and F and the Indian companies will be referred to as X, Y and Z. They are given letters in order to secure their anonymity and to be able to distinguish them from each other. Furthermore, a distinction is made between the Indian and Danish companies in order to be able to compare them. At the end of this section a table will be presented in order to illustrate the areas in which the case companies innovate.

Process innovation

Tidd and Bessant define process innovation as *"Changes in which they* (the offerings) *are created and delivered"* (Tidd and Bessant, 2009, p. 21). As such, the processes either lead to a final offering, delivering of the offering or supporting processes and can be both internal and external to the organisation.

At least two of the Indian companies (company X and Z) had implemented Lean in order to improve efficiency which can be categorised as an incremental process innovation; new to the company but known to the market. However, company Z explained that Lean was implemented upon wish from a customer, which can indicate that the initiative did not originate from a culture of innovation. The important point here is that, although having implemented process innovation, the companies might not be that innovative. This calls for caution if a Danish company is looking for an Indian company that is able to show initiative towards process innovation, as, even though the Indian companies seem to show ability to innovate processes, the initiative might be externally forced.

Company Y explains its process innovation more in detail. With every new project it splits the value chain into three parts; on location, near location and offshore location. This allows the company to analyse the process needed for the particular project and customise the process to it, thereby allowing new ideas to emerge for every project.

The Kaizen concept was also implemented in both companies. This displays some initiative to include blue collar workers in the innovation process, as Kaizen allows most employees to come with suggestions for improvements. How well used the Kaizen concept is, is however not documented.

The Danish companies in India also displayed different initiatives towards process innovation; company F has implemented Six Sigma and several of the other companies explicitly mention process innovation as one of India's strongest types of innovation. Company B states that innovation is about being more efficient, which indicates that in India innovation is primarily about optimising processes, i.e. doing process innovation.

It seems that Indian companies and Indian employees in foreign companies are naturally good at incremental process innovations. Danish companies cooperating with Indian companies or offshoring to India can use this information to consider if they should involve the Indian part in their process innovations.

Despite the facts mentioned above, there is room for caution. If the Indian companies are as good as they say at optimising their processes, why do Danish companies report that their Indian counterparts take longer to complete a similar task? However, this could also be due to cultural factors, but still relevant to take into consideration.

Product

Tidd and Bessant define product innovation as *"…changes in the things (products/services) that an organisation offers."* (2009, p. 21). This means a change to the current product/service offered by a company and can be either incremental or radical (Tidd and Bessant 2009, p. 21).

India is becoming one of the leading countries in the world in making 'invisible' innovations. These invisible innovations can be made by a simple housewife as well as a company (company A) and can be a process or a certain way of simplifying how things are supposed to be done.

Several major international companies decide to move their R&D to India (company A) in order to create a joined platform with their already outsourced production facilities, where R&D and production work together to develop faster implementation (Srivastava, 2011). For some companies, a part of R&D is moved to India to ensure the Indian employees' competences' are well used (company A).

The Danish companies C and D have R&D facilities in India which makes it easier to implement new ideas into their production units. Company D made a well-structured plan on how to implement the entire company setup before the outsourcing, which led to a lasting success.

Despite the extensive R&D facilities in India, there is a tendency of centralised control from Denmark or internationally, seen through the cultural pressure and initiatives.

Paradigm

Innovations in paradigms are defined as *"…changes in the underlying mental models which frame what the organisation does"* (Tidd and Bessant, 2009, p. 21). A paradigm innovation shifts the mind-set of what an organisation does or offers. For example how televisions or cars shifted from being viewed as luxury goods to being something most people can afford. It can be argued that paradigm innovations occur within the Danish companies as they adapt their culture into a mix of Indian, Danish and international cultures, thereby changing the mental model for how to do things in the company. An example is when company D moved operations to India. The Indian employees changed their culture over time into an international oriented culture, which slowly spread across the company's entire international operations.

Secondary research shows that 'inclusive innovation' is gaining ground in India. Inclusive innovation in India involves innovations that reduce the costs and increase the availability of goods, so the accessibility for the poor increases (Dahlman and Utz, 2007). This can be seen as paradigm innovations in the happening, as companies must shift their objectives towards a new segment, thus change their underlying mental models.

Paradigm innovations are difficult to observe, which means they can occur without the company or the public being aware. This has also made it difficult to identify paradigm innovations within the case companies. It is the type of innovations that companies pay least attention to, as they often are too comprehensive to manage proactively.

Inclusive innovation

Inclusive innovation in its purest form existed for many years, but the term inclusive innovation is fairly new and was first introduced by the World Bank in 2007. In addition to the 4Ps, this extra type of innovation is added to the analysis. This type of innovation is added as desk research as it is highlighted both by the Indian government (Innovation Council India, 2010) and in the literature about innovation in India. Since it was added on the basis of desk research, it has not been possible to find information about the local Indian companies or the Danish subsidiaries, and whether it is something they have been a part of or are thinking about being a part of in the future. It is, however, still relevant to include it, as it can contain great benefits for future investments in India. There is a big potential for numerous companies, as this type of innovation can be used in all developing countries in the world, and by being present in several markets, economies of scale can be reached. Furthermore it is possible for companies to increase their image and have inclusive innovation as part of their CSR programme, as this has been taking more ground in international companies worldwide.

Inclusive innovation is defined as the development of new goods and services for those who have been excluded from the mainstream development, and in India this group is the poor (Heeks, 2013). The core focus is on structures and processes required for developing innovation technologies, and the essential elements of inclusive innovation is to reduce costs and increase availability of goods, along with ensuring a sustainable livelihood (Dahlman and Utz, 2007). Foster and Heeks (2013) present four main aspects of 'inclusiveness':

- *Inclusivity of innovation precursors: for example that problems to be addressed by innovation are of relevance to the poor.*
- *Inclusivity of innovation processes: for example that the poor are involved in the development of innovative goods and services.*
- *Inclusivity of innovation adoption: for example that poor consumers have the capabilities to absorb innovations*
- *Inclusivity of innovation impacts: for example that innovative goods and services have a beneficial effect on the livelihoods of the poor*

(Foster and Heeks, 2013, p. 335).

Inclusive innovation can both be within product and process innovation. The term was first introduced by the World Bank in 2007 and created a shift in the paradigm of innovation (Chataway et al., 2013, p. 3). It has since received much attention from all over the world. The National Innovation Foundation of India (NIF) was set up in 2000 by the Indian government to provide support for grassroots' innovation and inclusive innovation (Innovation Council India, 2010).

Historically, NGOs and non-profit organisations have been the main drivers behind inclusive innovation and still remain a big source. There is great potential for multinational corporations to engage in this type of business (Chataway et al., 2013, p. 10). The drivers for going into inclusive innovation can vary, whether it is stagnation of the local market or high competition. Medium-sized companies or large multinational corporations can benefit from economies of scale through this type of innovation.

Cross company analysis

This analysis evaluates each company with a score from 1 (lowest) to 5 (highest), depending on the amount of focus put on each innovation type. The evaluation is based on a subjective estimation founded on the company data. The scores are given in relation to the subjectively evaluated average innovation levels in the investigated companies in Chennai. The average innovation levels of Danish companies are set as a subjective mean of the authors' experience with innovation in the Indian Companies. Score characteristics in relation to the overall innovation levels in the Indian companies are:

1. No signs of activities within the innovation type in question
2. Small amounts of unstructured activities within the innovation type in question
3. Initiated basic functional activities within the innovation type in question
4. Well-functioning coordinated activities within the innovation type in question
5. Widespread well-functioning coordinated activities within the innovation type in question

Table 3.2: 3P Company analysis

Innovation areas (scores from 1 [lowest] to 5 [highest])							
Company ↓	Product		Process		Paradigm		
Company A	Some industries supply lots of product innovations. Knowledge hubs (cinematic, IT etc.)	4	Innovation also means process innovation in India	4	India has pros and cons of current paradigm. Seeks to improve cons, and consulate trusts improvements in the future	4
Company B	Seeks to strengthen the product	4	Innovation definition: something that is more efficient than the current process	5	No direct innovation culture	2
Company C	Has plans on moving much R&D to India, indicating strong product innovation abilities	4	Moves R&D to India at a large scale, is a big process innovation, and indicates interest and abilities in innovating processes in general	4	Challenges aligning customer paradigms in innovation, but seeks to improve capability	3
Company D	Huge engineering group in India. Focus on cost cutting and technology development	5	Huge engineering group in India. Focus on cost cutting and technology development	4	Has an international culture. Has adapted (innovated) the paradigm from local to international in the Indian department at least (as one of the few companies)	4

Company E	Innovation box	3	Innovative techniques, innovation box. Process innovation is the strongest in India	5	Process innovation is the strongest in India, but tries to adapt	3
Company F	Product innovation, for quality products, and cost reduction	4	Big focus on process innovation	5	Tries to act as an international culture	3
Company X	Basic product innovation	3	Process knowhow can lead to innovation. LEAN implemented, but nothing else	3	Small signs of paradigm innovation	2
Company Y	Product specialisation - develops/combines new solutions to some extent	4	Re-invents process in on-site, near-site or offshore by splitting and assembling the value chain	5	Sends workers abroad to develop customer oriented paradigm, but still gap some places (selective partnerships)	3
Company Z	Invites customer to product development process, so has focus here. Adapts products in a smarter way to limit cost	4	LEAN implemented. Customers audit processes. New processes revolutionise products (drive shaft example)	4	Limited paradigm innovation	2

Process innovation is in focus in most companies, mainly due to cost-cutting. Product innovation is also in focus, which could relate to the heavily accessible R&D resources and a market oriented view which in turn relates to cost-cutting in many cases. Paradigm innovation is in focus to a lower degree. Only companies A and D exemplify or argue that paradigm innovation is successively in focus, with the rest of the companies trying in some degree to adapt to cultural paradigm changes at best. Danish companies considering moving innovation activities to India might obtain increased possibility of success within process and product innovation, due to the higher local focus and experience from working with these types of innovation. Companies requiring paradigm innovation in their outsourcing activities, should plan the whole process in detail, and might still not be successful with this innovation type.

Part conclusion

The above analysis shows that the Indian and Danish companies do well in both process and product innovation and primarily incremental innovations and paradigm innovations are present. There has been no evidence of position innovations, however these are probably present, just not visible without an extensive and resource demanding study. As an extension to the 4Ps, inclusive innovation is added to the analysis. This is not a new type of innovation, but differentiates from other types of innovation, since it focused on the part of the population with the lowest income in order to ensure their livelihood.

The findings of the analysis can be used as a preliminary guide to what can be expected of Indian companies with regards to innovation. The findings should, however, be taken with caution, as the sample of companies are few. Also, some of the information comes directly from the Indian employees. The Indian employees could be trying to look better in terms of innovation skills, in an effort to promote themselves to Danish companies, as they knew the purpose of our visit.

The above company analysis in Table 3.2 is based on a subjective interpretation of the notes taken through the company visits. This constitutes a natural bias of the scores shown. The bias was reduced by agreeing on the subjective interpretation, in a group of five persons that all visited the companies.

Other factors regarding innovation

This chapter constitutes an in-depth evaluation on each of the 3 Ps described in the previous chapter. The evaluation will focus on general advantages found in each of the 3 Ps in relation to India, and will ultimately conclude what to prioritise in a given business situation. The chapter also considers the origins of innovation and the presence of a creative climate required when innovating.

From where do innovations originate?

The previous chapter highlighted the degree of focus within each innovation type. In order to assess the advantages of each innovation more thoroughly, an investigation of the innovation origin has been carried out using Peter Drucker's '7 Sources of Innovation' (Tidd and Bessant 2009, p. 162). The seven sources are somewhat interconnected meaning that the presence of one source might lead to the presence of another. This in turn means that the borders of the sources can be somewhat vague.

Table 3.3: Innovation sources summarised

Company / 7 Sources	A	B	C	D	E	F	X	Y	Z
Demographic changes	X		X	X	X	X		X	X
New knowledge	X	X	X	X			X		
Incongruence (gaps to reality)	X				X			X	
Changes in industry/market structure	X	X	X		X			X	
Unexpected successes/failures	X								
Process needs	X	X	X	X	X	X	X	X	X
Changes in perception	X		X		X			X	

Source: Based on Tidd and Bessant (2009)

Company A stands out by the product/service it provides. Company A therefore sees all seven innovation sources as present within its business area. Company B focuses on knowledge sharing and needs from the market as innovation sources. Company C uses changed legislation and a changed perception view to create innovations. Also new market opportunities make for new process needs. Involving the customer in the innovation process creates new knowledge as well. Company D's innovation comes from demographic and market changes, also creating a need for new processes. Company E innovates based on a need to meet market requirements, especially cost cutting. This also requires new processes and leads to changes in perceptions. Company F focuses on cost cutting as a result of changing demographics in both Europe and India, resulting in requirements for new processes. Company X innovates through needs for new processes and newly gained knowledge. Company Y has market changes and especially the need for new and more efficient processes as the main innovation driver. The company is concerned with producing the same quality more efficiently. Company Z uses the market demands and thereby new process demands as innovation sources.

Overall it can be summarized that demographic changes, market and industry structure changes as well as process needs are major sources of innovation. Demographic changes as an innovation source can be explained by the large number of young people below the age of 25, as noted earlier. An extensive growth potential in R&D expenditure during the last ten years compared to other countries, an increase in internet and telephone access and the internationalisation of India in general, could also influence this source (Dahlman and Utz, 2007). As company A states: *"In 1991 India became a part of the open world and the world saw what India has to offer. This has resulted in the fastest growing market in the world."* This is an explanation of why market and industry structure changes are main innovation sources. The only source of innovation present within the investigated companies is process needs. This source can be seen as a result of changing demographics, changing markets and thereby new opportunities and changes in perception and gaps that require new processes. The companies aim at utilising India's potential within blue collar and low-wage white collar workers to rethink processes.

The outsourcing of departments to India can be entitled 'process innovation', but it also borders the concepts of product and paradigm innovation. Process need in an outsourcing-related context in India is thus naturally the central source of innovation.

Product innovation reflection

Utilising the seven sources of innovation requires an innovative workforce and a suitable innovative climate. The latter will be touched upon later.

The creation of an innovative workforce is strengthened by knowledge clusters. Both blue and white collar workers constitute strong knowledge clusters all around India (National Innovation Council). The clusters vary within anything from gems to textiles and IT. The extensive blue collar workforce along with great amount of new university graduates create competitive knowledge clusters that attract companies like B, C, D, E and F. Knowledge clusters consequently create a more innovative workforce, in turn stimulating product innovation.

In order to understand product innovation, it is important to notice that product innovation goes through three stages of a product life cycle. Based on the information given by the companies, most of these indicate signs of a fluid pattern. This means focusing on being market driven, looking at customer needs as a base of product development and re-design. They also tend to collaborate with experts in order to match the needs of the users (Tidd and Bessant, 2009, pp. 40-42). The five major industries of India (Surf India, 2013) are:

- Textile industry
- Indian retail industry
- Software industry
- Cement industry
- Steel industry

The common aspect of these five industries is the market driven need of product as well as process development, in order for them to exist to such an extent (Surf India, 2013). These industry clusters will also lead to beneficial competition on knowledge, leading to product development. This ensures that cluster companies can compete in the international market through, among others, product innovation, as they are used to even tougher regional competition.

Danish companies should understand that in order to gain success on the Indian market it is essential to have a network within the industry which they try to enter as well as an understanding of the mind-set of the Indian employees and what to expect from them (Ho, 2013).

Process innovation reflection

The focus on process innovation is supported by knowledge clusters as well. Cooperating with the supply chain and partners in the local area develops expert knowledge that can develop processes and attract new companies, like in the case of company B, C, D, E and F.

Process innovation can be present during the fluid phase in order to develop cost efficient manufacturing from the start and at the specific phase in order to improve the process design already in place (Tidd and Bessant, 2009, p. 40). The latter is usual for the Danish companies investigated, as the products are already in place in Denmark and only a part of the internal supply chain process is outsourced to India. As the companies establish and improve processes for existing products in India, usually with the purpose of cost reductions, most Danish companies consequently move parts of the product development including product innovation to India.

At least three of the Danish companies have large scale product development as well as production facilities in India, supported by process innovation both as an innovation source (Table 2.2, innovation sources summarised) and as an innovation area. Process innovation is crucial if companies are to survive in a competitive environment (Piper, 2008), with India's knowledge and labour conditions being an obvious choice for conducting process innovation activities.

Innovation in the specific (mature) phase is stimulated by cost reductions and quality improvement (Tidd and Bessant, 2009, p. 42). These two stimuli are focus areas of both the Indian and Danish companies investigated, meaning that a number of processes outsourced to India can be said to be in the specific phase. This phase is characterised by a high degree of process innovation and a low degree of product innovation, supporting that most investigated companies seek opportunities in process innovation through outsourcing and offshoring.

Paradigm innovation reflection

Paradigm innovation was lacking at focus levels within most of the companies. Most of the companies have either interests in initiatives, or already started initiatives in relation to cross country cultural paradigm alignment, but without major success. The challenges are many when moving the basic beliefs and values of people. An example of major non-cultural paradigm innovation is company D's development of relatively large R&D facilities in Chennai, restructuring many processes over a short period of time. Other successful examples of paradigm innovations were not found, making paradigm innovation a potential area of precaution for Danish and Indian companies looking for outsourcing ventures. Paradigm innovation can be connected with the psychological bias of the lower class in India. Company A described a middle class of 2-300,000,000 people, with the same buying power as Europeans. This number is rising steadily as the economy grows, but is limited by cultural mind-sets like the caste system.

This paradigm can be changed through paradigm innovation based on internationalisation and information, potentially allowing the economy of millions of people to increase (IFU). It could be a great opportunity for European businesses to utilise the rising knowledge levels in India as well as the large new market. As an example, Chr. Hansen, a Danish company, aims its growth strategy at the Asian low-income group and expects to experience income-increases during the upcoming years (Svansø, 2013). Another example to illustrate the increasing awareness of the growing potential in India is the Danish government's supporting initiatives on creating cooperation between the two countries (Udenrigsministeriet, 2011).

Paradigm innovation can be articulated through inclusive innovation (Dahlman and Utz, 2007). Developing a new paradigm through inclusive innovation in the low-level society is not enough, though. The middle and high level society must accept and participate actively in lifting the society, which could present a challenge, as the high social layers utilise the low social layers for profit.

What influences a creative climate

The creative climate is important for the idea generation and motivation when a company wants to include a certain group in innovation activities. An analysis of the creative climate is thus relevant. Tidd and Bessant (2009) have developed a list of components that are present in an innovative organisation:

A. Shared vision, leadership and the will to innovate
B. Appropriate structure
C. Key individuals
D. Effective team working
E. High-involvement innovation
F. *Creative climate*
G. External focus

This part will focus on F, creative climate, which involves a positive approach to creative ideas supported by relevant motivational systems (Tidd and Bessant, 2009, p. 100). Eight conditions under which creativity is stifled are identified. Each condition have been rated from 0 (innovation suppresser) to five (innovation thrive) in relation to a subjective data interpretation (Tidd and Bessant, 2009, p. 131) from the companies investigated. This will give a picture on how the creative climate actually inhibits innovation at these companies in general.

1. Dominance of restrictive vertical relationships: **2**
   Hierarchy both in terms of social rank, caste and professional rank influences the innovative climate in most companies visited. The only moderators are the few companies which tried to employ international culture standards, along with the personal strive to excel from many white-collar workers.
2. Poor lateral communications: **3**
   Lateral communications were functioning quite well in the companies

investigated. A general issue is, though, that Indians would preferably give you a satisfying answer even though it might not be truthful. This is especially the case when communicating across social or professional ranks.

3. Limited tools and resources: **4**

    The Danish-Indian companies visited are mainly at the Danish level of technology, because they are Danish subsidiaries. The Indian companies visited might lack a bit in technology, but lead in manpower resources to balance this.

4. Top-down dictates: **2** Top-down dictation is the standard in India, limiting creativity. The level of organisational silence among employees, as a result of respect for higher ranked employees or visitors, was increasing as the level of internationalization declined in the companies.

5. Formal, restricted vehicles for change: **3**

    The Danish-Indian subsidiaries in many cases had tools and formal systems for innovation. The extent might not be as comprehensive as in Denmark, but it was found in most companies. The Indian companies saw innovation more as small improvements and were overall lacking behind the Danish subsidiaries regarding formal innovation structures.

6. Reinforcing a culture of inferiority: **2**

    The strive to excel and distinguish oneself from the masses is a driver for change and innovation in India. It is limited by top-down restriction and dictation. Below the surface, the drive to excel is an egoistic motivator triggered by cultural heritage and pressure to climb the professional latter and receive respect and wealth. This could be triggered by fear from being inferior, as the whole society is hierarchy focused. Again only few of the international companies pull up the score by trying to avoid this bias.

7. Unfocused innovative activity: **3**

    This score is split as well. The Danish-Indian companies seem to structure activities better than the local Indian companies. At the Indian companies, innovation is triggered by coincidence or customer demand and seems not to be focused in any specific direction. Within the industries in which India is to some extent market leader, the innovation might be more focused to keep up with local competition and keep the market leader position.

8. Un-supporting accounting practices: **x**

During data collection there has been no focus on accounting practices leaving this score unfilled and excluded from the calculation below.

The average score is 2,7 indicating that the climate is not that innovative from a subjective perspective. The pros of the climatic conditions are the amount of resources (labour) available and striving to excel through outperforming amongst white collar employees although stimulated by egoistic desires. The cons are the top-down dictation, creating restrictive vertical relationships and a culture of inferiority.

Part conclusion

Process and product innovation are areas of focus for both the Danish and Indian companies investigated. It is not recommendable to focus solely on one of the innovation types when outsourcing to India. A recommendation for both types is specific to the situation.

The analysis reveals how process need is related to demographic changes, market changes and perception changes and is the main source of innovation. Process innovation was also identified as the main innovation type in focus. Theory suggests that cost-cutting and quality focus are elements of the specific phase in the innovation lifecycle (Tidd and Bessant, 2009). A majority of both the Indian and Danish companies investigated has a similar focus, suggesting an interest and foundation for process innovation in India. Theory also suggests that preliminary process innovation has cost-cutting capabilities within some industries (Tidd and Bessant, 2009). Process innovation in India can be summed up as recommendable mainly for companies having mature products in which processes can be optimised with a cost focus.

Both product and process innovation are supported by the immense white and blue collar workforce, as they are supported by knowledge clusters that enhance the worker innovation degree. White collar workers are the main sources of product innovation whereas product innovation is also shared with the blue collar workers to some extent.

The analysis indicated that product innovation is recommendable for companies having products in the fluid phase of the innovation lifecycle, as the R&D knowledge for product development is comprehensive in India. A considerable number of the companies investigated has a customer or market oriented focus, which is a distinctive characteristic of the fluid phase. Product innovation is recommendable within well-developed industries like software, textile and steel procreating knowledge cluster synergies. Product innovation in India can be summed up as recommendable mainly for companies requiring new products which can be optimised according to the market.

Paradigm strategies are partly an element worthy of precaution but mainly an opportunity that can be exploited if understood and utilised correctly, breaking down cultural and societal barriers to grow through inclusive innovation initiatives. A complete paradigm innovation on all social levels is thus necessary to obtain further increased market and labour advantages. A focus on developing a new paradigm in the Indian society and economy is of increasing interest to Danish companies. It is recommended that Danish and Indian companies follow the situation and contribute to this paradigm shift to yield the long-term benefits. The subjective evaluation of the climatic conditions influencing innovation leads to the conclusion that Danish companies must be aware of the lack in conditional stimuli the less internationalised the department/company in India. In particular the Danish companies must be cautious of top-down dictation causing restrictive vertical relationships and a culture of inferiority, which increased as internationalisation declined. The table of innovation sources is based on a subjective interpretation of the notes taken through the company visits. This constitutes a natural bias of the data shown. The bias was reduced by agreeing on the subjective interpretation in a group of five persons.

Conclusion

In order to uncover the opportunities that Danish and Indian companies can obtain through cooperation, a thorough analysis was carried out on the drivers of innovation and the areas within which innovation can take place. The analysis was carried out on data obtained through nine company visits in Chennai, India, balanced with theory and data obtained from secondary literature. The following outcomes served as a guideline for both Indian and Danish companies seeking insight in new cooperation opportunities with regard to India. The results of the analysis can help Indian companies gain an understanding of strengths and weaknesses of their business environment. The Danish companies might be inspired as to areas in which innovation could be strengthened by cooperation with India, but also in which areas innovation is likely to be cause troubles.

Through the theory of Innovation Drivers, the analysis identified an increasing political support on innovation, through focused campaigns, designated innovation councils and legislation moderation in favour of cross-national cooperation. A result of this innovation support and increasing internationalisation initiatives is economic, technological and educational growth. The new technological opportunities within communication serve as a huge advantage in information sharing, both locally and globally. A huge opportunity lies within the lower social class as well, which could make for a whole new market. It was identified that products must be adapted to this segment and to the population in general through product re-design and possibly inclusive innovation. The growing population of India, and the growing middle class, might also call for innovation within the green solutions area due to scarce resources creating conflicts. Prohibitions of innovation drivers were identified as economic inflation and the political system, which is still old-fashioned, bureaucratic and corrupt, though changes are initiated.

The analysis identified the presence of all four innovation types – product, process, position and paradigm innovation. Process innovation is the most common innovation type used through the investigated companies. This is a sign of companies typically being in the specific phase of the life cycle in which cost-cutting and quality is in focus. It was also evident that the local Indian companies are focused on incremental rather than radical innovation. It was suggested that cross-country cooperation within process innovation can be highly advantageous in many industries, if the process re-structuring is prepared and implemented meticulously. Danish companies should be aware that the Indian company has self-initiated innovation initiatives, meaning a true interest in acting at parallel innovation levels, before partnering up though. Product innovation was also used in most companies, through especially R&D departments. It is suggested to consider cross-country cooperation within product innovation in industries where knowledge hubs can be found, as for example in steel, textile and IT industries. Limiting product innovation to those strong industries strengthens the chances of a beneficial cooperation.

A driver for product innovation worth noticing is the extensive number of engineers being educated each year, making a cheap, highly skilled product development knowledge foundation in the industries highly possible. As many companies already have production in India, a synergy effect can in some cases also be obtained by having product innovation located near the production site. Product innovation outsourcing is also recommended in the fluid phase of the life cycle, where a new company requires initial product development with the help of engineers that are less costly in India. Paradigm innovation lies in re-designing the whole mind-set of the socially divided Indian society, restraining a huge market from acquiring a beneficial education giving buying power and supporting the knowledge level of India. This is closely tied to the concept of inclusive innovation, including all societal layers when innovating to gain maximum outcome. The recommendation of paradigm innovation is addressed in Indian companies and the Indian society to increase the living standard and national growth. A consistent pattern of the investigation is that the level of internationalisation of the Danish or Indian subsidiary in India is closely connected with the success of innovation. The higher the internationalisation level, the more successful the innovation initiatives could seem to be. Extensive differences in culture and terms of working seem to be diminishing the feeling of unity though crossing borders, constituting a bias for cooperation on innovation initiatives through the organisation.

CHAPTER 4

Knowledge Management

Henriette Kolbeck, Thorsten Søgaard Krægpøth, Lasse Skov & Christopher Wulff

Abstract

The purpose of this chapter is to inform the reader how to conduct effective Knowledge Management when sourcing business processes to India. When doing business in India it is crucial to establish a foundation of trust between the organisations and to develop a setup that proactively supports effective knowledge sharing. By analysing empirical data collected in India, this chapter will outline the most important aspects of establishing effective Knowledge Management between Danish and Indian companies.

Introduction

The economy of today's world is no longer just focused on material items and tangible assets. Globalisation and the ever more common practice of outsourcing and offshoring business processes from Western countries to low-cost countries influenced a change in how companies view assets. The industrial economic focus has changed to a focus on knowledge economy and companies are now talking about the importance of gaining and nurturing knowledge assets (Boisot, 2010, pp. 1-7). Previously Western companies decided to outsource/offshore departments with focus on physical labour; now many companies also now recognise the value in outsourcing/offshoring knowledge-based departments like parts of or even the entire research and development division. This focus on knowledge among other things helped launch the practice of Knowledge Management. This involves the creation and mobilisation of knowledge both inside and outside the company boundaries. In order to reduce the distances between divisions and network partners, it is important that knowledge is transferred, shared and optimised.

Knowledge cannot be transferred in the same way as material items, which can be as easy as a parcel delivered at your doorstep. It becomes even more difficult when the transfer must be across cultural, educational or language barriers. If the company wants to optimise the use of its knowledge assets, it will have to find out how to ensure that knowledge is nurtured properly and flows throughout the company to be available to all involved parties.

In order to establish how this is best done, the following questions will be investigated and answered.

- *Which knowledge management strategy should be used, when offshoring or outsourcing to India?*
- *Which focus areas are important when transferring knowledge to your partner in India?*

Methodology

In this assignment the focus is on Knowledge Management and in particular knowledge sharing within a Danish-Indian context. For this purpose, a literature review of the subject is being conducted as well as a field trip to Chennai, India. In Chennai, nine companies were visited. The companies are a combination of Indian- and Danish-owned and they operate in the areas of manufacturing, engineering and IT. For the purpose of this assignment the Danish companies will be named Company A-F and the Indian companies will be called Company X, Y, and Z upon reference.

The assignment will begin with a review of the conceptual ideas of Knowledge Management within the context of knowledge transfer and knowledge sharing in order to create a common consensus of the subject. Two knowledge management strategies are presented, and the chapter will focus on finding the most appropriate strategy when sourcing to India. A quick look at the cultural implications for knowledge sharing will also be taken, as it is too important to leave out when considering the context. Hereafter the focus will be on relevant topics of knowledge transfer and knowledge sharing within a Danish-Indian context. Here the focus will be on empirical data from the company visits, but some theoretical frameworks will also be included when appropriate. Then the two different strategies will be related to the findings. The function of the expatriate and the relation to being a knowledge transfer agent and the importance of having the correct organisational structure will be included. This will lead to some technical suggestions on how to build a successful knowledge base, and in the end, some general recommendations for Knowledge Management in an offshore or outsourcing project to India will be presented.

The Knowledge Management concept

Knowledge management is a young and emerging concept that holds many different definitions and approaches. In his book 'Knowledge Management: An integrated approach' Ashok Jashapara (2011) has gathered and divided the different definitions in to two groups.

"Some literature on knowledge management is heavily information systems oriented, giving the impression that it is little more than information management. Other literature looks more at people's dimension of knowledge creation and sharing, making the subject more akin to human-resource management" (Jashapara, 2011, p. 10-11).

As this chapter is focusing on knowledge sharing and transfer, a human resource process perspective is adopted. Furthermore this perspective offers two different definitions. In 1999 Swan et al. defined knowledge management as *"…any process or practice of creating, acquiring, capturing, sharing and using knowledge, wherever it resides, to enhance learning and performance in organisations"* (Jashapara, 2011, p. 13). The same year Skyrme suggested this definition: *"The explicit and systematic management of vital knowledge and its associated processes of creating, gathering, organising, diffusion, use and exploitation, in pursuit of organisational objectives"* (Jashapara, 2011, p. 13). As the goal of offshoring and outsourcing knowledge related products and processes should be to be in control of the management of knowledge and having a systematic approach to this is seen as important, Skyrme's definition is adopted and used for the remaining part of this chapter.

In his book on knowledge management Jashapara also presents two knowledge management strategies. The strategies are chosen because they are the two most commonly practiced. They are presented as a continuum between a codification strategy, which is described as technology-led, explicit knowledge oriented and with the focus on codifying knowledge, the use of databases, and high turnover; At the other end of the continuum is the personalisation strategy, which is people-led, tacit knowledge oriented and with the focus on engaging in dialogue, channel expertise, and high profits (Jashapara, 2011, p. 105). The two strategies are not mutually excluding and elements of both can be used, but it is important to have a clear orientation to one or the other, as the focus of the knowledge management strategy otherwise can be muddled.

Sharing knowledge

When considering either outsourcing or offshoring important business processes to India, any organisation has to be aware of the pitfalls in relation to sharing knowledge. It is not simply enough to come to terms with wanting to share knowledge; one has to know exactly which knowledge is shareable and how it is shared in an inter- and intra-organisational context and culture.

When it comes to sharing knowledge, organisations have to be conscious about the difference between the organisation's and the individual's willingness to share knowledge. A pitfall could be that the organisation as a whole wants to share knowledge, but the individuals might find it difficult to share sensitive information. As an example, one might consider an engineer who holds tacit knowledge directly related to his performance and payment. If he shares that knowledge and thereby makes it explicit, he might sacrifice his own performance for the purpose of the organisation. He might not be willing to do so.

In the context of globalisation and global competition, organisations expand their boundaries towards new markets, both in collaboration with other companies outside their own hierarchy in the form of outsourcing and inside their hierarchy in the form of offshoring. By doing so, companies can obtain competitive advantages, by collaborating with supply-chain partners or other companies, who can add value to the products and/or services in the global market.

Cross-disciplinary, cross-unit, and cross-organisational collaboration leads to situations where sharing competitively sensitive information is necessary in order to achieve organisational goals (Boughzala and Briggs, 2012, p. 1).

When people in the organisation share knowledge with each other, they agree upon mutual trust. If a person possesses personal knowledge, he or she might not be willing to share that knowledge without the appropriate amount of trust. Looking at inter-organisational knowledge sharing, the trust between to individuals is even harder to achieve.

Boughzala and Briggs (2012) define the share-ability of private knowledge between individuals in an inter-organisational context as follows: *"The share-ability of a set of private knowledge is defined as the degree to which one feels willing to reveal that knowledge to people who are not members of one's own organisational unit"* (Boughzala and Briggs, 2012, p. 9).

An individual in the organisation may believe that some knowledge areas are highly shareable with one partner, but difficult to share with others due to the lack of trust between the latter (Boughzala and Briggs, 2012, p.9). It is given that the organisation needs to be aware of this knowledge sharing conflict in order to obtain a successful knowledge sharing, both in intra-organisational and inter-organisational context.

Boughzala and Briggs (2012) conducted a qualitative empirical research on the degree to which individuals in inter-organisational collaboration are willing to share knowledge with each other, and which kind of knowledge is shareable. The research shows qualitative findings from an exploratory field study of 16 organisations. From this research, the authors constructed a framework, which can be used to illustrate the issue of shareable knowledge (see Figure 4.1).

Figure 4.1: Value framework

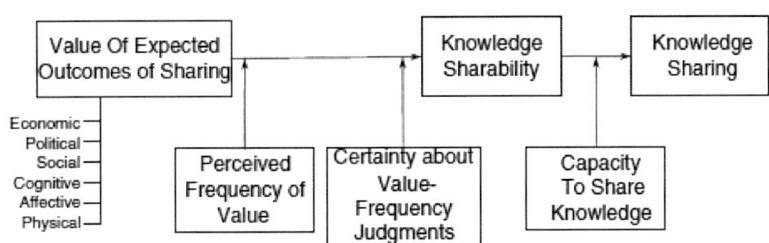

Source: Boughzala and Briggs (2012, p. 10)

The unit of analysis of the framework is not the organisation itself but the individuals. It is in general not the organisation which is not willing to share knowledge. A manager might instruct the organisation in how to share knowledge, but if the individuals are not willing to share the given information, it will be hard to achieve a successful knowledge sharing system. Furthermore, the framework suggests two areas that the organisation has to be aware of to achieve its knowledge sharing goals. The first one, which has already been highlighted, is "knowledge share-ability". Knowledge share-ability is the extent to which individuals are willing to share knowledge with each other on the behalf of mutual trust. In other words, knowledge share-ability is about the attitude among individuals.

The latter area is "knowledge sharing". Knowledge sharing should be understood as behaviour among individuals in the organisation. Knowledge sharing is *"… said to occur when group members voluntarily exchange knowledge with the purpose of reaching a broader understanding of their group goal and its accomplishment"* (Boughzala and Briggs, 2012, p. 10). According to the way in which Boughzala and Briggs formulate the two concepts, we now understand that there are two factors that the organisation needs to be aware of.

Looking at the framework, we will see that the value of the expected outcome of sharing knowledge deals with six types of value; *Economic, Political, Social, Cognitive, Affective and Physical value.*

Economic value is the monetary value which can be obtained by teams, departments and individuals when sharing knowledge within or between organisations. More explicitly, the economic value refers to the extent to which individuals will receive monetary value for sharing knowledge.

Political value refers to the extent to which individuals can gain status and power by sharing knowledge.

Social value between individuals can be a great advantage among individuals. If an individual holds important information about significant processes in the organisation, he or she will have the opportunity to be recognised as an important staff-member between knowledge sharing partners.

Cognitive value refers to the value of developing one's own potential. A positive outcome of sharing knowledge is learning more and developing working skills. If one has a negative cognitive value from sharing knowledge, he or she will not be willing to share.

Affective value is the emotional value that one might achieve in sharing knowledge with co-workers. It can be perceived as the happiness of sharing or the opportunity to help others.

Physical value should also be considered. If the physical ability to share is non-existing e.g. meeting opportunities, IT-systems etc., knowledge sharing will not be successful.

Perceived frequency of value determines the overall sense of how often value would be realised. Certainty about value frequency judgment determines the likelihood that one's value-frequency judgment is correct – Is it correct that I will receive the value by sharing knowledge? The perceived frequency of value is therefore a belief of how much value one would get from sharing knowledge. The certainty about value frequency is a judgment one makes to be sure of whether one would achieve the perceived value after all. The capacity to share knowledge is the individual's intention to act. It will only be carried out if actors are capable of executing the intended action. They will only be able to do so, if they are able to use tools such as software programmes, which make it possible to physically share the knowledge (Boughzala and Briggs, 2012, p.11).

It is important to have in mind that even though the manager or the organisation wishes to implement effective knowledge sharing systems, knowledge sharing will only be successful, if the individuals of the organisation are willing to share. Various considerations should have the focus of the organisation, and both the ability and the willingness to share are important areas to understand. Practical solutions could be team-orientated incentive systems or rewarding actual knowledge sharing through IT-systems.

When both the mind-set and physical systems are in place, it is time to look at how to transform individual tacit knowledge into explicit shareable knowledge.

The importance of transforming tacit knowledge into explicit knowledge

Before an organisation is able to transform tacit knowledge to explicit sharable knowledge, it needs to understand the difference between tacit and explicit knowledge. Tacit knowledge only exists in the mind of the individuals in the organisation, and has yet to be formalised. An example is an employee who has knowledge about a product or customer that only he knows. Knowledge which is only accessible for one individual or a small group of individuals is defined as tacit knowledge. Explicit knowledge has already been formalised and made available for the organisation, and is shareable through for example IT-systems. Raw data, construction manuals, turnover etc. are examples of explicit knowledge.

The challenge of a company who is looking to either outsource or offshore certain business processes is to transform tacit knowledge into explicit knowledge in order for both organisations to benefit from it.

Figure 4.2 below is created by Alavi and Leidner (2001) and illustrates the transformation of tacit knowledge into explicit knowledge between individuals.

Figure 4.2: Transformation of tacit knowledge into explicit knowledge

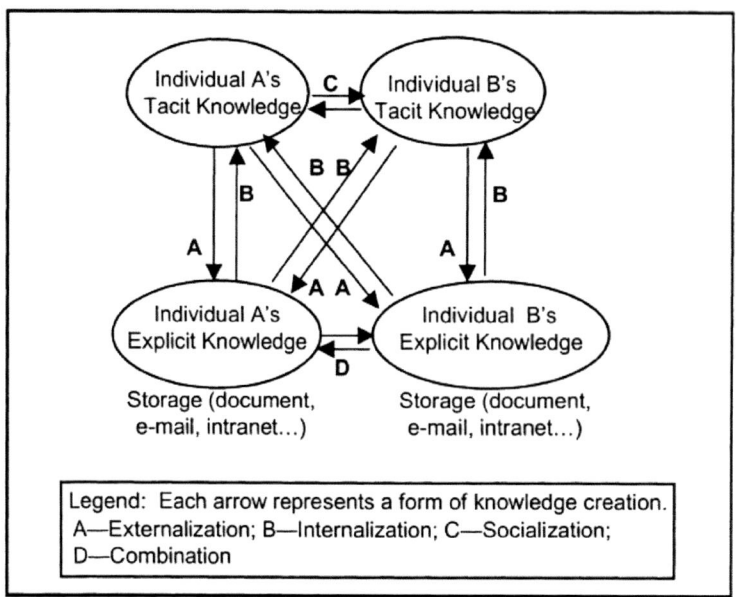

Source: Alavi and Leidner (2001, p. 117)

Figure 4.2 illustrates what is meant by tacit knowledge and how it is transferred into explicit knowledge. It is meant as a guideline to show how sharing knowledge in different ways may not be as useful as many companies believe.

Individuals in organisations gain knowledge through work processes. The knowledge they gain might be shared with other individuals in the organisation, but not through formalised processes. This does not make the knowledge explicit. This is shown in the figure above and is called *socialisation*. The knowledge shared is still tacit and to transform this into explicit knowledge, it has to be formalised and made available to both organisations and all employees. This is called *externalisation*. This process could be done through It-systems such as intranets and various forms of online available documentations. This will be further discussed in the section "IT-systems as tools for knowledge sharing". The preferred situation is called *Combination* where all individuals in both organisations are willing and able to share their explicit knowledge, i.e. that individual A and B has made their knowledge explicit by for example contributing with written statements through an intranet or in another way making their knowledge accessible to other people in the organisation.

When individuals do not share knowledge, there is a risk of sub optimisation in both intra- and inter-organisational context. Think of a salesperson having information about a customer. He might know about the customer's preferred delivery terms, product designs, quality specification and demand patterns. Because elements of his salary concern commission, he might not be willing to share this information with the rest of the sales personnel, because he is afraid of losing parts of his salary. When engineers design new products, they would be interested in knowing details such as customers' preferred product designs, delivery times and so forth. Therefore, by working with team-oriented bonus systems instead of personal commissions, companies can overcome the risk of sub optimisation. Furthermore, by expanding the bonus system to involve the whole organisation or outsourcing/off-shoring partners, companies ensure that employees share knowledge and work together across silos to achieve their common goals.

When outsourcing or offshoring to India, the company should consider optimising its incentive systems to support common goals of interest. In order to be successful in working with knowledge sharing between organisations in Denmark and India and thereby ensuring that the partnership works towards common goals, the manager has to consider the differences in culture, time-zones and behaviour in Danish and Indian companies.

Cultural distance in relation to knowledge sharing

For the purpose of examining what effect the cultural distance between Denmark and India has on Knowledge Management and in particular on knowledge transfer and sharing, two concepts of distance have been adopted: "Spatial dispersion" meaning the distribution of the knowledge sender and recipient in space and "Contextual differentiation" being the distance culturally, linguistically and professionally of the knowledge sender and recipient (Ambos and Ambos, 2009, p. 10). The spatial dispersion between Denmark and India is evident. With the two countries being almost 6,000 kilometres apart it is obvious that there is a large distance, which naturally limits physical meetings and thereby face-to-face knowledge sharing. In their research Ambos and Ambos (2009, p. 21) conclude that especially geographical distance will have a negative effect on knowledge transferring from person to person. It is not just physical availability that hampers with transfer of knowledge, but sender and recipient must also be available in time. An Indian employee has less holidays and work longer hours compared to their Danish counterparts. Several of the visited companies mentioned that employees have had problems with contacting their Danish colleagues, because the Danish employees were not available (not working), which resulted in a delay in the Indian employees' work.

In regard to the contextual differentiation, companies wishing to outsource or offshore to India also have a great challenge. When taking a look at the linguistics the country has more than 1,600 languages (Meganathan, 2011, p. 2), but English is an associate official language and almost compulsory second language. Indians seeking higher education must therefore speak English (Meganathan, 2011, p. 26). In general companies can communicate with Indians in English, but issues of communication might arise due to troubles of understanding certain dialects, but that is both from Indian to Dane and vice versa as was found out when visiting Indian companies. The Danish dialect can be very hard to understand. Professionally it is important that all parties involved in knowledge sharing and transferring are skilled to understand knowledge, not just the meaning hereof but also how to use it, because that is the real value.

Like the way in which cultural holidays and traditions influence Danes' availability in time, cultural distance also shows its effect on knowledge transfer in businesses in different ways. All differences cannot possibly be explained, but some examples will be presented. When seeking to outsource a company, one will often look for a partner in India and it is important to understand how India is a culture of relations. Establishing a good relationship and creating trust is very important. Company A, an Indian company, explained that it found it important to clarify how both companies benefitted from a partnership, and that the company was very much interested in knowledge sharing as long as a contractual agreement was in place. In companies B and C it was important in order to accept a partnership, that there should be long term benefits for the society and that the company should not replace Indian workers with Danish ones. When deciding to offshore it is also worth bearing in mind that as to sub-suppliers there are requirements from the Indian government saying that one should choose sub-suppliers within India. In general the politically unstable situation in India should be considered when choosing India as the country for an offshoring or outsourcing business process. Due to changing governments, decisions relating to governmental affairs can be changed back and forward and may hinder the company severely.

The poor infrastructure makes technical solutions for knowledge sharing and transfer even more important. It is also a good idea to check the access to resources. Have in mind that due to the challenged Indian electric grid, a continuous influx of power is not present. Back-up generators for IT-systems are a must. Direct threats to the effectiveness of knowledge transfer can also be found in how Indians handle feedback. In company E both Indian employees as well as the Danish manager acknowledged that due to their culture, Indians found it difficult to receive and give feedback which naturally limits knowledge sharing and creation. As a polite people, Indians do not like to disappoint others and saying no, which means that it can be difficult for a Dane to know if the Indian colleague has understood the knowledge that was being shared. As a specific example from company E: when the Danish manager visited a site in India, it took a day for the manager to understand that a number of the employees he had addressed did in fact not speak English. When it came to seeking knowledge, the manager also noted that due to cultural backgrounds the Indian employees were more reluctant and sat waiting in their offices for it to come to them, while Danes acted more proactively.

When looking at the cultural and linguistic distance, Ambos and Ambos (2009, pp. 21-22) found evidence that to influence the effectiveness of knowledge transfer within personal relations, this distance has to be minimised. On the other hand they did not find empirical evidence supporting their theory, i.e. that cultural distance influenced technical means of knowledge transfer. This led them to conclude that for shorter geographic and cultural distances, personal means of knowledge transfer are recommended, but the more distance rises, the more technical means should be the preferred way to increase knowledge transfer effectiveness. As stated by Ambos and Ambos (2009, p. 28) *"We found that firms should carefully adjust their transfer mechanisms to the distance between sender and recipient in order to achieve the most effective knowledge transfer."* These findings from Ambos and Ambos actually suggest that companies should use a codification strategy when approaching knowledge management. The choice of knowledge management strategy will be researched further.

The importance of Knowledge Management when sourcing to India

To ensure optimisation of business processes, financial success and smooth outsourcing or offshoring processes, it is important to have focus on proper Knowledge Management. Through the empirical research collected during the visit to India, several important themes have come up that need to be further explored and analysed. The following section will deal with the empirical findings from India in relation to Knowledge Management. An analysis as to what extent they have been successful and how companies can further develop their competencies regarding Knowledge Management will be conducted.

From the empirical data collected in India many important aspects have been discovered that directly indicate the importance of Knowledge Management. The most important aspects, besides making a profit of course, that a company needs to focus on when considering sourcing business processes to India, are presented in the following. Using expatriates has also been a major success for many of the companies. Therefore an entire section has been devoted to this subject. Among the most important aspects are:

- Building trust
- Continuous training of Indian employees
- Understanding the difference in managerial styles from Danish to Indian companies
- Developing a long term relationship
- Achieving organisational transparency through data sharing

The areas above are not much different from what Danish companies desire when working together. The major difference is that when sourcing to India, these areas are not as "easily" fulfilled. When wanting to gain a desired competitive advantage through outsourcing or offshoring to India, Knowledge Management is an important tool that can be used to support the fulfilment of the mentioned aspects.

Conducting proper Knowledge Management can be a way of showing the Indian company trust while still keeping control. All of the Indian companies want to share knowledge more effectively in order for them to trust their partners and to ensure the continued development of a long term relationship. From the experience in India it is clear that the Indian companies have a distinct advantage, when it comes to further developing business processes and physical products, because they have an entirely different approach to solving problems. Furthermore, organisational transparency can be gained by sharing data across organisations, manufacturing management, organisational management and innovation.

The companies that were visited all try to achieve the above mentioned areas, some more effective than others. The common denominator is *effective Knowledge Management*. It is not simply enough to share data either through seminars, training, It-systems etc. As a company that is looking into sourcing to India, one must ensure being able to transform whatever knowledge the company has, into a form that the Indians can benefit from.

The following section will deal with the specific initiatives that have been implemented by the companies visited in India. The initiatives will be explained, analysed and finally judged on how effective it has been and where improvements can be made. This will be the background for the final recommendations to which areas any company should focus on, when sourcing to India and how to approach them.

Sharing knowledge from a Danish company to an Indian company

As stated, many of the companies included in this research, are working with Knowledge Management in order to achieve greater success in India. This section will analyse the initiatives launched by these companies in order to accomplish effective Knowledge Management. The empirical data collected stems from six Danish companies who have sourced to India and three Indian companies who have experience with working with foreign companies.

From the experience gained by the six Danish companies, who have successfully sourced to India, the following table shows some of their suggestions or actual implementations on how they managed the important aspects mentioned previously in the section "The importance of Knowledge Management when sourcing to India." It is important to know that successfully dealing with these aspects, is what the research group considers to be effective Knowledge Management. Obviously there are several other aspects that contribute to the success.

Table 4.1: Effective Knowledge Management in India

Important aspects that needs attention	Building trust	Continuous training of the Indians	Managing different managerial styles	Developing long term relationship	Achieving organisational transparency through data sharing
Company A	Share operational plans, managerial tools, and general sensitive information.		Make sure to have native Indians in the management to ensure better communication top-down.	Invest money and assets to convince the Indian company that you mean serious business.	Use of intranet to share data
Company B	Hire Indian workers or develop their skills rather	Develop the Indians skill sets.	Teach the Indians to give feedback.	Share sensitive data.	Use of intranet to share data

		than employing a foreigner.				
Company C	Have held "Supplier day" where all suppliers meet up and share experience s.	Have used both Danish and Indian cultural ambassadors.	Create an environment that stimulates input from the Indian employees. E.G by giving out financial bonuses or recognition from the top management.	Make sure that you are contributing to the society in whatever business you work in.	
Company D	Has earned a lot of trust by giving out many titles to the Indians.	Has had several seminars to ensure that the Indians can actually use the data shared by the Danish company.		The seminars held has contributed to building a long term relationship, because the Indians appreciate the investment made.	Has created a digital portal called "The Idea portal" where all employees can contribute with an Idea.
Company E		In order to enable the employee feedback the company has weekly meetings around a whiteboard where the statuses of all projects are shown by the help from the "Traffic Light Model."		Sharing data through their digital portals.	Uses a digital platform called "8 Tools", "Lesson learned" and "Lynch" for project management, sharing knowledge and knowledge transfer and to ensure the teams across both companies have a communication platform.
Company F	Has earned trust by nurturing global corporation and actively encouraging the Indians to give feedback and share their knowledge.	Has a global management team that travels around the departments in order to train them.	The global management team has a lot of focus on teaching the Indians to give feedback and that it is OK to disagree with the management. They are trying to break down the very steep Indian hierarchy.		Through a digital portal called "My online voting" any employee can vote on a project they believe to be a good investment for the company.

The dimensions in Table 4.1 are created from the research questions that were answered during the visits to the companies in India. The five outlined dimensions above proved to be the areas on which the companies had greatest focus.

As shown there are numerous examples on how Danish companies have tried to develop a proper base for effective Knowledge Management. Though one aspect that stands out from the empirical data; namely that only one company, company D, has invested time and training in ensuring that the Indians can actually utilise the data that is shared. As mentioned earlier, a major cultural difference is that the Indian has issues with saying no. Therefore it is extremely important to point out that when a company tries to establish effective Knowledge Management, it has to continuously ensure that the Indians are actually using the databases, reading the material given and contributing with their own tacit knowledge through the digital portals etc.

However, knowing what other companies currently try to do to overcome the challenges with effective Knowledge Management is not enough. One need to look into what the Indian companies are actually doing themselves and what they believe will create real value in a partnership.

Use of knowledge in the Indian companies

Although the major experience and developments within the area of Knowledge Management have occurred in Western industrialised countries, many Indian organisations have acknowledged the importance of Knowledge Management and have started Knowledge Management initiatives (Sanghani, 2009, p. 3). It is therefore also important to include an Indian perspective. Three Indian companies form the base of the empirical data collected during the research. Though only one of the companies has had experience with Danish companies, all companies still have valid and important points in relation to how to share knowledge. All three companies function as suppliers for larger, Western organisations, and when wanting to partner with an Indian company they underlined the importance of being involved in the customers' innovation and development process. An involvement of this kind can be through visits to the customers' facilities, where the Indian companies learn about the customers' processes by direct observation or by the customers sending expatriates to them in order to train them in the processes needed. For this kind of arrangement to be successful a good knowledge sharing system should be organised, and limiting your partners' access to given information, involving the processes you want them to learn, will hinder a successful outcome of the partnership and minimise trust from both sides. Company Y stipulated that the lack of trust previously had caused a partnership to stop.

At a more low-tech level the Indian companies look to Japanese management techniques for improvement, like Kaizen. Company X set up an opportunity for improvement suggestions from all employees at a white board easily accessible in the factory. It will work as a way of minimising the distance between top and bottom of the organisation, when employees feel that they have a possibility to influence the organisation, and it can be a direct source of new knowledge. When setting up these opportunities it is important for management to follow up on the suggestions; otherwise the purpose of the "suggestion box" will be diluted.

One final and very important note from the Indian companies is that no matter whether you choose to outsource or offshore to India, you must not try to make the company Danish. It is crucial for the Indians to feel that they work and belong to an Indian company. They are open to suggestions and changes that can help them become more successful but only as long as they do not lose their identity. All companies visited whether purely Indian or Danish companies who have sourced to India, all agree that having Indian representatives in the top management is crucial.

The personalisation perspective

In this section two elements of a successful personalisation strategy will be researched. These two elements are chosen due to their relations to being person-led and ability to be tacit knowledge-oriented. These elements are the expatriate function and the training of the subsidiary towards becoming a part of a learning organisation. Chang et al. (2012) argue that choosing an expatriate with good knowledge transfer skills as well as improving a subsidiary's absorptive capacity is vital elements in securing a high subsidiary performance. Therefore a closer look at the expatriate as the knowledge transfer agent as well as the organisation set-up will be taken.

Using expatriates - understanding of expatriates in a HRM perspective

When choosing to source activities from Denmark to India, there is of course a major gap in the way people think, perceive and perform. One of the elements in creating a successful sourcing process is bringing in an expatriate as the extended arm of the focal company. The expatriate can be an important tool in transferring tacit knowledge and engaging in a continuous dialogue. Sending a person abroad to work in the same company is not just a matter of ordering the flight ticket and start working with the same issues as back home. When identifying knowledge management as an important element in the sourcing process, matching the expatriate with the company's expectations to the level of knowledge transfer is vital. Chang et al. (2012) examine whether the ability-motivation-opportunity framework in connection with knowledge transfer can be related to the success of the subsidiary. The researchers define the dimensions as:

"…expatriate ability refers to the knowledge, skills, and experience needed to solve difficulties in transferring knowledge. Expatriate motivation refers to the willingness to devote time and to persist in solving difficulties in transferring knowledge. The transfer of knowledge occurs in a social context, and resources and opportunities for transferring it often reside in social relationships…" (Chang et al., 2012, p. 929).

The researchers conclude through empirical findings that knowledge transfer is more successful when the expatriate's knowledge transfer skills, motivation and opportunity are high. It is also concluded that the success of the subsidiary and the knowledge transfer are positively influenced when the focal company has focus on developing the subsidiary's absorptive capacity (Chang et al., 2012, p. 944).

When sending an expatriate to India a company should focus on finding an employee that is able to and motivated for building trust and developing a long term relationship, to involve themselves in continuous training of Indian employees, to learn about the differences in managerial styles and to share data. One of the long term advantages of having an expatriate is the breakdown of the geographical distance barrier, but furthermore the expatriate should be able to break down barriers to effective knowledge transfer like cultural, linguistic and educational barriers. At the same time, the company should also give the expatriate the opportunity to do so by creating an organisation that can absorb the knowledge through organisational learning. Absorptive capacity is defined as *"…a firm's ability to utilise externally held knowledge…"* (Jashapara, 2011, p. 147) The next section will focus on elements in creating this absorptive capacity.

Organisational structure and absorptive capacity

Jashapara (2011) presents two relevant concepts. One is organisational learning defined as *"Organisational learning means the process of improving actions through better knowledge and understanding"* (Jashapara, 2011, p. 133) and the other is team learning. Team learning is an integrating process, which creates shared understanding and interactive systems, whereas organisational learning is more institutionalising with the focus on creating new routines and a diagnostic system. An important element of organisational learning is information distribution also known as knowledge sharing, meaning that one of the end goals of information distribution is the creation of new knowledge. Team and organisational learning are two concepts that are important elements in enhancing the absorptive capacity of an organisation. Therefore, companies should not underestimate the value of team training.

Another important issue in influencing and furthering a knowledge sharing culture in a company is taking a look on the organisational framework and how this fit with your intention to implement Knowledge Management systems (Sanghani, 2009, p. 12). As described briefly earlier, culture has an important impact on knowledge transfer and management style and the hierarchical breakdown of the organisation is culturally conditioned. Like the findings present there is a large difference in managerial style and organisational structure.

When wanting to increase the effectiveness of knowledge transfer, it is essential to minimise the distance between sender and recipient, and it is therefore important to limit the links between the two. Indians tend to have high focus on titles, there is a clear respect between manager and subordinate and the communication channel is mostly vertical. In Denmark there has been a focus on more horizontal communication channels within knowledge creating companies. Horizontal communication channels aid in making sure that as little as possible gets lost in translation. A more flat hierarchy will also give more responsibility for the individual employee and ensure that he or she will have more influence on the work itself, which in the end should help create a more motivated and committed employee. A flat hierarchy represents a bottom-up, emergent strategy and the *"...process is typically characterised by the creation of organisational cultural infrastructure to enable continuous information sharing, knowledge renewal, and creation of new knowledge"* (Malhotra, 2002, p. 13).

The different styles of communication channels are illustrated in the model below. The model displays two ways of aligning resources through different points of interconnection. On the left is shown "the Butterfly" where different departments only communicate with the other organisational counterpart. An example hereof can be company E. The Indian offshore project functions as a supplier to the main office in Denmark. If the company choose to align resources through this model, the Indian company's sales department would only communicate with the Danish procurement department. No other lines of communication would be involved. If this was the case, the company could experience longer lead times. The chain of links expands which will slow down communication time and increase risk of losing vital information (e.g. master data and transactions data). Therefore when starting up a new sourcing project in India it could be beneficial to adopt "the Diamond"-approach (see Figure 4.3). Here the communication flows between all departments creating numerous points of interconnections, which can increase the speed and accuracy of the communication and the ultimate goal to reduce lead time. This was also the approach adopted by Company E.

Figure 4.3: The Butterfly – diamond model

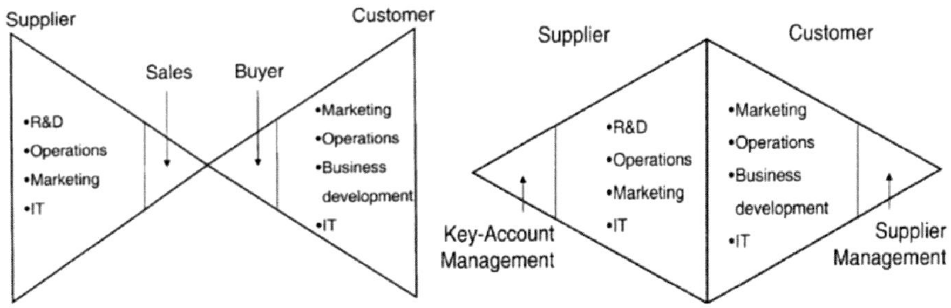

Source: Christopher and Jüttner (2000)

Upon start of a sourcing project it is important to respect the hierarchy culture of India in order to not patronise their systems and show the people working within them respect. It might be the ultimate goal to marry the two styles or wanting the Indian department to completely adopt the Danish style, but one should be aware that in order to be successful, the company should teach the employees the foundations of the desired communication style. This includes training technical capabilities as well as personal motivation. For some Indians it might be stepping over a boundary when critiquing a superior, or not involving him or her in all communications with other departments; therefore proper training hereof will assist in the overstepping of boundaries. It is suggested, when doing a sourcing project to India, to start with the aspects in the Butterfly model and slowly move towards the diamond model, as the organisational culture changes.

A company sourcing in India will rarely expect the project to be a complete success from day one. In fact it might even take many years for the project to meet expectations or in the end it might fail completely. Creating a success when trying to integrate the Danish communication methods is a matter of partly changing a cultural perception of how communication best flows throughout the organisation and will take time, so patience is of the upmost importance. Some pitfalls in relation to structural changes can be:

- Lack of a specific boss to report to, which creates confusion and possible power struggles among management. Indians are generally used to a clear chain of command.
- If setting up a large department in India it can be a struggle to adapt the flat structure, unless the company divides into smaller, more manageable units.
- A flat organisation tends to produce a lot of generalists but no specialists, because the specific job function of employees might not be clear.
- As titles and powerful positions are very important in India, a lack of respect in cross-functional communication might emerge which could devaluate the information shared.

Therefore in an effort to create more effective communication and knowledge sharing one might lose other important organisational aspects. Several of the Danish companies visited underlined the importance of having cultural ambassadors. The representative from Company C said that the company previously had success with these ambassadors, and that *"...they unfortunately had been discontinued"*. Selecting both employees in the focal organisation and in the department in India to learn about the different cultures, both with organisationally and cultural purposes, and using these trainees to influence their colleagues in the desired direction. Therefore cultural ambassadors could help the transition go smoother.

In order to minimise confusions it will also be an advantage to work with clear job functions. These should be easily accessible through e.g. an intranet. This will help the employees to find the right colleagues for assistance on any project and form a basis for the division of responsibilities. Indians also like to work with a clear working schedule when it comes to e.g. deadline, number of employees involved in a project and a budget. A structured approach to a work schedule could be a good compromise when trying to contain some of the chaos involved in a flat hierarchy compared to a tall one. Due to cultural elements human resource management is generally a very important organisational element in India. So establishing a strong and competent HR department is vital and an important foundation for creating a knowledge sharing culture. Research shows that *"The human resources departments are well positioned to ensure the success of Knowledge Management programs, which are directed at capturing, using and re-using and re-using employees´ knowledge. Through human resources management a culture that encourages the free flow of knowledge for meeting organisational goals can be created"* (Soliman and Spooner, 2000, p. 1).

When implementing changes at an operational level it will be natural to consider different change management models.

The codification perspective

In the previous section elements of the personalisation perspective were examined. Next, various tools in the implementation of the codification strategy will be discussed, as the findings showed that data sharing was found important by the companies in Chennai.

Building a successful knowledge-base

In order to share knowledge between individuals and organisations, the implementation of an IT-based system would be beneficial, because it allows the individuals to share their knowledge with the rest of the organisation.

This section of the book proposes different tools to help the manager establish a successful knowledge-base, thereby making information, data, skills etc. available.

As mentioned earlier in the chapter, when dealing with cross-cultural partnerships, organisations seldom have the opportunity to share knowledge by face-to-face methods such as meetings because of the geographical distance. IT-based systems will therefore be a natural choice, when managers want to ensure effective knowledge sharing across a geographical distance.

It is important to understand that IT-systems only function to the extent that knowledge is being uploaded to the system and regularly updated. If the organisation does not allocate resources to ensure that the knowledge-base is regularly updated, they risk that employees, relying on the knowledge in the systems, fail in important aspects of their jobs. Company

E pointed out that one of their main problems with Knowledge Management was the lack of employee ownership of documents, and the documents were therefore not properly updated. Furthermore, employees have to be trained in using the different systems in their everyday job-function. However, this subject is outside the scope of this chapter.

The literature in the area suggests numerous approaches to knowledge sharing techniques. Both non IT-based systems such as cross-functional project teams, Knowledge Management training and education, storytelling and mentoring and IT-based systems such as intranet, extranet, data warehousing, data mining, decision support systems and content management systems, to mention a few.

In the section below, different systems for creating effective knowledge sharing between Danish and Indian companies will be proposed.

IT-systems as tools for knowledge sharing

As briefly mentioned in this chapter, when establishing partnerships between Indian and Danish companies, one should have in mind the knowledge sharing culture in the partner organisation. Indian knowledge-based companies, companies that are not only manufacturing companies, but companies which practice knowledge-based processes like engineering to order, Research & Development etc., are already using different IT-systems for knowledge sharing. One should have in mind that Danish companies are further ahead on the subject of using knowledge sharing IT-systems than Indian companies in general, but knowledge-heavy organisations such as company Y are already trained in using such systems, but this is seldom the case.

The Danish company will probably have to teach the Indian companies to use these IT-systems, feed the systems with data and update the system on a regular basis with the newest information.

Data warehousing

A data warehouse is a collection of electronic data from various sources, organised to allow you to create reports and analyse data. As an example, it can be used by an organisation, which wants to collect data on its production unit's costs, sales, stock prices or any other basis for decision making.

This type of IT-system will come in handy, when the manager wants to control or measure activities in the Indian partner organisation as well as the focal organisation. The system is suitable for both offshoring and outsourcing activities. When the Data warehouse has been created and data have been uploaded, the manager is able to filter different data and make cross references and tables, which makes the data visual and thereby useful as a basis for decision making. This enables proactive response to situations that do not work out as planned.

Data warehousing allows the organisation to measure and act on everything that can be physically measured, thereby making it a useful tool in working with Indian companies, who do not already use IT-systems for knowledge sharing.

Data mining

As databases grow larger and data become complex, it can be a difficult task to precisely measure the desired performance numbers. This is where Data mining becomes relevant. Data mining denotes the search for patterns and structures in large amounts of data.

Through for example algorithms or direct observation, data mining systems try to find relationship between data points in order to visualise and utilise the complex information.

Data mining systems should be considered when making use of data warehousing or other forms of database systems for decision making or performance observations.

Content management systems (CMS)

A Content Management System is a piece of software that helps to organise and facilitate cooperation, create documents and other information, and through which individuals or groups can handle a volume of electronic content, such as documents, manuals, images etc. The content management system is usually an easy to use piece of software that makes it easy to share files between organisations. The use of content management systems makes it easy for the Indian company to share its explicit knowledge with the rest of the organisation and with the Danish company. The user-friendly nature of the systems makes it easy to learn.

ERP and CRM systems

An ERP system, or Enterprise Resource Planning system, is a software programme that handles the majority of a company's functional areas. ERP integrates all business functions such as order processing, sales and marketing, purchasing, stock management and accounting etc. ERP systems are built up around databases and will also need a variety of data inputs from every employee working with these functions. The advantage from this kind of system is that the manager will be able to collect all functional business operations in the same software programme, allowing him to get an overview of e.g. the company's performance and costs. By introducing the ERP system in the Indian company, information regarding functional areas such as stock management will be transparent for the relevant employees.

A CRM system, or Customer Relationship Management system, enables the company to keep track of relationships and transactions with its customers. The CRM system collects, processes, shares and uses knowledge about customers. If the Indian company handles customers or uses customer information in regard to product development processes or similar customer oriented business processes, the CRM system should be used to share customer knowledge with the involved organisations, to make it simpler to gain the necessary customer knowledge. A CRM system can be integrated in the ERP system under the sales and/or marketing function.

One should keep in mind that any IT-based system for knowledge sharing needs to be maintained regularly by auditing, updating and uploading data in order for the system to function successfully. Furthermore it is important to be aware of the challenges in establishing a knowledge sharing culture which is often a time-consuming and resource-heavy project. But the more time spent and resources allocated, the more likely a result in higher performance in business processes and faster product development in partnerships between Danish and Indian companies (Taylor, 2013, pp. 81-82; Soliman and Spooner, 2000, p. 338)

Implementation of IT-systems for knowledge sharing

"…technology is the "pipeline and storage system for knowledge exchange" but of itself is not Knowledge Management" (Soliman and Spooner, 2000, p. 337). This quote is an example of how the area of Knowledge Management has changed its focus in literature. It is worth noticing that even though IT-systems can be a helpful tool for successfully implementing Knowledge Management, the manager needs to have in mind that human aspects are important as well. One of the main tasks in implementing Knowledge Management systems is to gain access to tacit knowledge, as has been discussed earlier in the chapter.

Focus on the Knowledge Management strategy

Before getting involved with Knowledge Management systems, the company needs to be aware of the costs concerned with such projects, especially in the start-up phase.

It is necessary to formulate a strategy for the Knowledge Management project in order to allocate resources and to set up goals to ensure that everything goes as planned. During the strategy phase, the organisation must consider how to capture tacit and explicit knowledge, and with whom the responsibility lies. Soliman and Spooner argue that organisations should focus their resources on tacit and explicit knowledge as a 80:20 rule, meaning that managers should not concentrate the same amount of energy on both areas at once, because of the risk of failing by doing so. To determine whether it should be tacit or explicit knowledge that receives the greatest amount of resources, the organisation needs to know the following listed in Table 4.2.

Table 4.2: Determination questions

1. The market
2. The profitable areas
3. Whether the organisation provides one-off solutions or the same solution repeatedly.

Source: Soliman and Spooner (2000, p. 339)

If the company offers solutions to its customers, primarily involving repeating business processes, then it should focus on aligning resources to capturing, automating and harnessing explicit knowledge. This means that the organisation should invest heavily in IT-systems such as the ones highlighted in this chapter.

If the company offers one-off solutions (products or services that are not repeated or reproduced), it needs to focus its resources on actions that concern tacit knowledge, e.g. hiring the best experts available.

No matter whether the Indian partner company concentrates on one-off projects such as engineering-to-order or focusing on repeating already invented solutions, the manager needs to have in mind where the resources should be allocated before engaging in implementation.

In order to implement a know-how strategy for knowledge sharing in the partnership, a research conducted by Price Waterhouse Coopers in 1999 shows seven different factors to have in mind. See Table 4.3.

Table 4.3: Price Waterhouse Coopers' seven factors

1	Focus only on what the business needs to know, i.e. become knowledge focused
2	Make important knowledge visible, i.e. become knowledge visible (e.g. create and make explicit pathways to the experts and important wisdom within the company)
3	Pay attention to the vocabulary of knowledge, i.e. become knowledge defined (e.g. customers' needs versus customer feedback)
4	Go beyond the company to tap knowledge from customers, suppliers and competitors, i.e. become a knowledge seeker
5	Make it clear to employees that knowledge sharing is a core value for the company, i.e. become a knowledge culture
6	Measure the results of the implementation of the Knowledge Management programme, i.e. become a knowledge assessor
7	Reward the sharing of expertise and intelligence, i.e. become knowledge exemplified.

Source: Soliman and Spooner (2000)

The above factors could easily be used as a checklist to make sure that the strategy covers all elements of both the Indian and the Danish organisation when implementing Knowledge Management systems.

The support of Human Resource Management

As mentioned earlier in the chapter, the organisation needs to focus on the incentive system which directly stimulates the behaviour of the employees regarding knowledge sharing. For example, if the employees receive parts of their salary based on time spent on knowledge sharing activities, they are likely to spend more time on these activities. However, incentive systems are not the only aspect to have in mind when trying to engage the employees in knowledge sharing. According to Soliman and Spooner, there are at least seven initiatives supporting Knowledge Management activities. See Table 4.4.

Table 4.4: Seven supporting initiatives

Social gatherings of staff	In some organisations talking to colleagues may be considered a non-value-adding activity. The human resources department could facilitate staff meetings to support Knowledge Management activities.
The office layout	The layout of spaces for staff to meet informally is important to encourage exchange of ideas and share knowledge. The human resources department could team up with management to create office space for staff Knowledge Management meetings.
Trust between employees of the firm.	In general, increased trust between employees improves the chance of

	Knowledge-sharing. The human resources department could play a role in building trust among staff so that they can share knowledge.
Differences in culture and language	Clearly the more languages employees speak the better their ability to acquire knowledge of customers and markets, especially in global markets. The human resources department through its role in recruitment and staff development could assist in selecting employees with appropriate cultural and linguistic backgrounds to support Knowledge Management activities.
Timeliness	The timing of the Knowledge Management effort is important for its success. The timing of facilitating support for Knowledge Management activities by the human resources department could increase the success of the program.
Learning and mistakes handling	If employees are encouraged to discuss their mistakes openly, a culture of "openness and seeking help" could lead to the creation of a learning organisation. The human resources department could assist in creating a learning environment far from fear of punishment and penalties. This could in turn facilitate the Knowledge Management activities.
Senior management involvement and support.	The inclusion of senior management in the Knowledge Management effort provides additional motivation for employees to share knowledge and increases the chance of success of the Knowledge Management programme. The human resource department's assistance in motivating employees could lead to increasing support for Knowledge Management activities.

Source: Soliman and Spooner (2000, p. 340)

The initiatives in the above table are guidelines as to how to successfully implement knowledge sharing in and between organisations. These initiatives should be considered when formulating the Knowledge Management strategy.

This section of the chapter has been concerned with the fact that IT-systems need a Human Relations Management approach in order to function properly.

Implementing IT-based Knowledge Management systems

When implementing new tools, processes and activities in organisations, there are numerous approaches for the way in which it should be implemented. This chapter focusses on a simple tool called the "PDCA Wheel".

Figure 4.4: The PDCA wheel

Source: Michelsen (2010, p. 9)

The PDCA wheel focusses on four phases of implementing improvements in an organisation. In the "planning" phase, the organisation determines the desired improvements. When implementing knowledge sharing systems, the organisation needs to determine which IT-systems are best suited for the Knowledge Management strategy formulated by the organisation. In this phase it is also necessary to determine which actions need to be taken in order to fulfil the Knowledge Management strategy mentioned earlier in this chapter.

In the "doing" phase, the organisation is actually implementing the Knowledge Management systems. In the "checking" phase, the organisation measures whether the determined actions and goals have been met. In the "action" phase, the organisation seeks to maintain the changes made, so that employees do not fall back into old patterns.

The PDCA Wheel is accompanied by the SDCA Wheel (see Figure 4.5), which seeks to standardize the new working patterns concerning the knowledge sharing systems. By standardizing working patterns, the company can "rotate" the PDCA Wheel again to further improve the Knowledge Management system and employee attitude towards the knowledge sharing culture.

Figure 4.5: The SDCA wheel

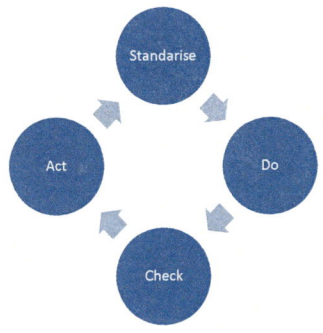

Source: Michelsen (2010, p. 10)

Conclusion

When considering engaging in Knowledge Management activities it is crucial to have focus on the individuals of the organisations and their ability and willingness to share information. It is not simply enough to formulate a vision in relation to sharing knowledge, and any company considering sourcing business processes to India will have to create the right circumstances for effective Knowledge Management. Team and inter-organisational incentive systems could work as a solution to overcome sub optimisation issues e.g. rewarding Knowledge sharing activities. To further support effective Knowledge Management, managers need to know how to support the transformation of organisational tacit knowledge into easily accessible explicit knowledge.

Unlike the Danish culture, in which it is common to give feedback no matter what status one has in the hierarchy, Indians do not have the same mind-set. One should consider the cultural differences and the hindrance it can cause when trying to implement effective Knowledge Management. Continuous training and supporting the Indian employees is central for inter-organisational Knowledge Management to succeed.

When sourcing business processes to India, the empirical research has shown five important aspects to consider in order to achieving effective Knowledge Management. These are building trust, continuous training of Indian employees, understanding the difference in managerial styles, developing a long term relationship and achieving organisational transparency through data sharing. Many of the companies have created digital platforms in order to share knowledge between the organisations and others have used cultural ambassadors to train both Danes and Indians in the cultural differences.

Theory implies that the cultural distance between India and Denmark would suggest a codification strategy, but findings showed that human relations are important in an Indian company. Therefore, when sourcing to India, Danish companies should adopt a more personalisation oriented strategy in which expatriates can be an important element. Making the right choice of a person to go to India is important from many aspects, not just purely technical and educational skills. The personalisation strategy should still be rooted in a strong technology base. Knowing the issues and various important aspects of the attempt to share knowledge across company boundaries such as transforming tacit into explicit knowledge will help one create the optimal IT-system to support sharing information. IT-systems worth considering are CRM systems and ERP-systems. These systems are useable when sharing knowledge in inter-organisational context, but also important is the Knowledge Management strategy that helps ensure reaching the goals of the company.

CHAPTER 5

Outsourcing or Offshoring?

Jeanette Holm and Mette Husum Dalstrup

Abstract

This chapter focuses on the globalisation, the drivers hereof, and a discussion of the different globalisation strategies. Should companies outsource or offshore to enter the Indian market? Using Dunning's OLIE model and the PESTEL analysis this chapter seeks to investigate which globalisation strategy is more suitable for the Indian market. Two companies are chosen and used as cases. The chapter examines the two companies' owner specific advantages and examines whether or not the companies implemented these in Chennai. Furthermore, the chapter identifies the location specific advantages and challenges of doing business in India and examines if there is a difference depending on the company being a manufacturing or a knowledge company. Finally, reflections are made on the theoretical framework (OLIE) and thereby discussing the sustainability of this model.

The drivers for globalisation

Globalisation is a phenomenon frequently discussed today and has increasing influence on the company's choice of strategy, localisation and so forth. Globalisation is characterised among other things by the increasing trade between countries. This is to a large extent caused by the fact that it has become cheaper and easier to communicate across borders. Due to globalisation, more countries go through an economic development. In this regard the BRIC-countries are good examples (Carlsen and Jensen, 2008). This development makes it more attractive for Western companies to expand (in some way) into these new markets.

India has become an attractive market for Western companies, including Denmark. Statistics show that in recent years the Danish export to India has increased (Udenrigsministeriet, 2012). As a result of more export, more companies have decided to enter the Indian market. This includes both manufacturing as well as knowledge companies. (Dansk Statistik, 2013) When companies decide to take advantage of the increasing globalisation, they have to choose a globalisation strategy. When discussing such a strategy you need to include the terms of offshoring and outsourcing. These terms will be defined later on. There are, however, different drivers for outsourcing and offshoring. According to Sanders et al. (2007) three different drivers are important for choosing outsourcing: economy, resources and strategy. The economical drivers will often be the prospect of cost minimisation due to for instance lower wages. The resource drivers will be the possibility of tapping into some knowhow, which the company lacks, or to gain access to raw materials. Finally the company can be driven by strategy, which is often the possibility to enter a new market.

For offshoring, Peeters (2007) acknowledges that cost drivers still are a prime justification, but companies are more and more interested in offshoring because of the strategic possibilities. It is crucial for the companies to consider the pros and cons of both strategies before making a decision on how to globalise. Furthermore, it is vital that the company knows what its owner specific advantages are. If this is not clear prior to the company's market entry, the company might, by accident, outsource some of its core competences without knowing (Prahalad and Hamel, 1990). In order to establish the pros and cons of doing business in India, two cases have been selected, based on the character of the companies. One is a knowledge company and the other is a production company. The choice has been made to investigate if there is a difference in the evaluation process in relation to making the decision on how to globalise dependent on the type of company. Both cases used the globalisation strategy internalisation when entering the Indian market and both are Danish companies. This leads to the following research questions:

1. *What are the owner specific advantages of the two case companies?*
    a. *How do they ensure that these are maintained in their departments in Chennai?*
2. *What challenges do companies face when doing business in India?*
    a. *Is there a difference depending on whether the company is a manufacturing company or a knowledge company?*
3. *Is it appropriate for the two cases to have chosen an internalisation strategy for the Indian market?*

Definitions

To distinguish between outsourcing (externalisation) and offshoring (internalisation) the following definition has been chosen according to Arlbjørn et al. (2013, p. 18):

Outsourcing: Relocation of activities/jobs from Denmark, thus these will be managed by a third party by its own ownership, management and control

Offshoring: Relocation of activities/jobs from Denmark to another country while ownership, management and control is sustained.

In order to distinguish between a manufacturing company and a knowledge company the following definition is used throughout this chapter:

Manufacturing company: A company that produces a physical product

Knowledge company: A company that generates knowledge/services as a main product.

Literature review

In this paragraph, the chosen theory will be presented. The overall framework for this chapter will be Dunning's eclectic paradigm with elaboration by Teit Lüthje, OLIE. Furthermore, the PESTEL analysis will be used to describe the location-specific advantages in India.

OLIE

Originally, the OLI-model was created by Professor John Dunning. The OLI-model is, from a holistic view, a summary of various theories gathered into one. The model is specifically related to the emergence of multinational companies. It is important to understand that the OLI-model is an analytical framework which can be extended according to the need for further analyses. According to Dunning's eclectic paradigm the internalisation of a company's activities depends on three factors: "Ownership-Specific Advantages", "Location-Specific Advantages" and "Internalisation-Incentive Advantages" (Dunning and Lundan, 2008, p. 95-111). The above mentioned factors illustrates why it is called the OLI-model.

Ownership-specific advantages

The ownership-specific advantages largely consist of intangible assets but it is not given that only these can be specified as being owner-specific. The advantages take the form of something that is unique for the company, when it is crucial to maintain control of these assets. Therefore the owner-specific advantages can take the form of both intangible as well as tangible assets. According to Dunning there are three basic types of ownership-specific advantages (Dunning, 1993, p. 101). The first type consists of property right over e.g. raw materials or immaterial assets as for instance product innovation, brands and patents. The second type reflects the company's ability to manage and coordinate several geographically spread activities in various countries. Finally the third type covers the formal and informal institutions that govern the value-added processes both within the company as well as between the company and its stakeholders (Lüthje, 2011, p. 14).

Depending on the type of a company's unique resource, strength and ownership-specific advantage, the need for protection and control may vary. Therefore the importance of clarifying the ownership-specific advantages is great when deciding on the globalisation strategy to be used.

Location-specific advantages

Location-specific advantages incorporate the advantages achieved by delegating parts of or the entire production to another country. Hence these factors determine if it is more advantageous for the company to place a manufacturing unit in the host country rather than to maintain the production in the home country and continue to export – hence the concept offshoring (Lüthje, 2011, pp. 14-15). The location-specific advantages could for instance involve specialisation of labour, known as comparative advantages. Thereby the advantages are determined by the countries' factor endowment and hence by differences in wages and productivity and thereby differences in unit labour costs. Furthermore, the advantages could include access to raw materials, minimised transport costs in connection to geographically proximity to the market and trade barriers such as tariffs and import quotas.

When identifying the location-specific advantages there can also be factors that may affect the localisation negatively. The company must consider these as well. To name a few these could include cultural differences such as language barriers as well as business culture, business traditions, lack of knowledge revolving legislation, corruption and bureaucracy (Lüthje, 2011, pp. 14-15).

Internalisation vs. externalisation advantages

The underlying basis of internalisation is the ownership-specific advantages which the company may intend to protect and control by establishing a subsidiary. As mentioned, these advantages are unique, and when a company is facing risks in terms of e.g. imitation of knowledge or technology, the internalisation advantages increase.

The need for internalisation might also occur, if there is no established market in terms of various suppliers. It will limit the company's possibilities for globalising if the company cannot outsource activities due to the lack of existing providers (Lüthje, 2011, p. 16).

The term Foreign Direct Investment (FDI) is frequently used when discussing internalisation. A FDI occurs when a person or a company owns a minimum of 10 percent and thereby has concurrent influence on companies' abroad (OECD, 1999, p. 8). A FDI could also be based solely on financial investments. There are two kinds of FDI's, the traditional kind of mergers or acquisitions, and the so-called Greenfield investments where companies establish for instance a new factory (Lüthje, 2011, p. 18).

Additionally, there are four objectives of FDI that are consistent with the OLI advantages described above. Firstly, there is *resource seeking FDI* which aims to benefit from the host country's natural resources such as minerals, raw materials and lower labour costs. Secondly, there is the *market seeking FDI* the purpose of which is to identify and exploit new markets. Thirdly, *efficiency seeking FDI* (global sourcing FDI) seeks to achieve an efficient allocation of international, economic activities within the company so it benefits from differences in product and factor prices and to diversify risk. Finally, *strategic assets/capabilities seeking FDI* aims to acquire existing companies and thereby protect the owner-specific advantages in order to uphold the company's global competitive position (Lüthje, 2011, p. 18).

In response to Dunning's OLI-model in its origin, Teit Lüthje has extended it by adding externalisation as a globalisation strategy choice – hence OLI(**E**) - and the term outsourcing. Outsourcing involves all activities which are managed by an external business partner. The motives driving the choice of outsourcing may among others include the lack of knowledge regarding the market, a wish for proximity to the market and probably the foremost frequent motive, cost-minimisation. The minimisation in costs is reflected in the operations as well as in the start-up of involving a business partner rather than setting up a new facility. To provide a visual overview the OLIE-model is displayed below.

Figure 5.1: The OLIE model in brief

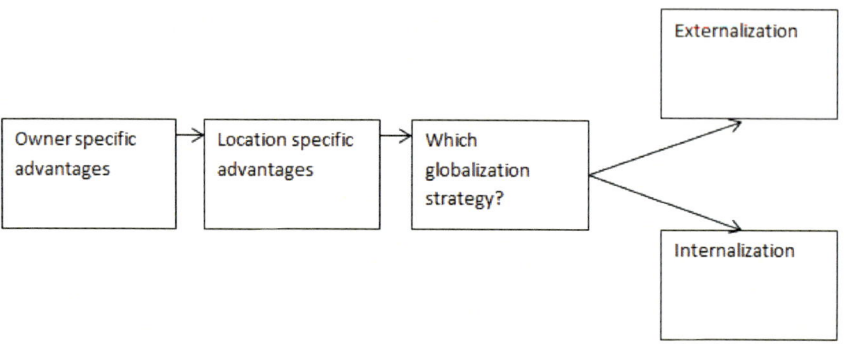

Source: Based on Lüthje (2011)

The cons of outsourcing could involve minimisation of control; hence the external business partner has main control of the delegated activity. As a result of less control, the risk for imitation also occurs in connection to this globalisation strategy.

PESTEL

For the specification of the locations specific advantages the PESTEL analysis will be used. This analysis is categorised in six different factors which are political, economic, social and cultural, technological, environmental and legal. These will be elaborated below.

The political factors involve taxes of the country as well as regulations in the labour market, the political systems and so on. The economic factors consist mostly of the conditions of the financial state, the inflation, interest rates, currency, GPD and wage levels. The third factor being addressed in the analysis is the social and cultural factors. These include lifestyle, values, education level, demography of the population and income distribution. The technological factors involve the grade of innovation, the technological development and so forth. The environmental factors are of increasing significance and therefore also mentioned here. The underlying issues are energy consumption, waste distribution, green financial statements and corporate social responsibility. Finally, the legal factors are examined, among others legislation, competition, imports and exports as well as legislation in respect to the labour market. Overall, the PESTEL analysis will help create an overview of India and its population and consequently help determine the location specific advantages for both manufacturing and knowledge companies (Kotler et al., 2010).

Delimitation

This chapter is based on a field study in Chennai, South India. Therefore, any reference to India will be to the Southern part of the country. It was decided to focus on one manufacturing company (Company C) and one knowledge company (Company E) to answer the research questions. However, the remaining companies will be included in the analysis when appropriate.

Dunning's eclectic paradigm with elaboration by Lüthje (2011) will be used as the framework of this chapter. Since the two case companies have already decided on and implemented their globalisation strategy, OLIE will be used as a tool for reflection rather than an advice for the two cases. Companies reading this chapter may, however, use and reflect on the information as a guideline for doing business in India.

The PESTEL analysis will be used only in respect to gaining an overview of India and will therefore not be used as a specific strategic analysis. Furthermore, not all issues of the PESTEL analysis will be discussed, only those relevant for the purpose of this chapter. Due to the length of this chapter PESTEL will be drawn as one model (identical for both production and knowledge).

Methodology

Ten companies were contacted and visited during the week in India. The companies were both Danish and Indian. Before going to India, we prepared questions for each company. These questions were answered through semi-structured interviews and observations. This method was chosen in order to be able to follow up on any questions. The interviews were recorded and one group member took notes during each interview. After returning to Denmark, the interviews have been summarised. In addition to the interviews the company spokespersons gave us an introduction to their company and showed us around the facilities. After returning to Denmark further information (secondary literature) about the two companies in question was gathered. The companies will stay anonymous and will therefore be referred to as company A, B and so forth.

If more cases were considered, it would strengthen the reliability in the research. The argument for focusing on two cases is to enhance the differences that might be applicable no matter whether it is a knowledge or a manufacturing company by comparing these two continuously. The selection criteria were also based on the grounds that this chapter seeks to investigate the globalisation process of international companies located in India. The Indian companies visited are therefore not considered to such great extent.

The two companies

In order to create a clear understanding of the two cases being used in this chapter, the below table has been drawn up. It shows five different factors and how these differ depending on the two cases.

Table 5.1: Short description of cases

	Case company C	Case company E
Knowledge or production	Manufacturing	Knowledge
Annual turnover	34+ billion DKK	7,6 billion DKK
Number of employees	23.000+	10.000
Globalisation strategy in Chennai	Internalisation (offshoring)	Internalisation (offshoring)

How to maintain the owner specific advantages

In this section the owner specific advantages will be identified for both case companies using both the semi-structured interviews and research conducted after returning from India.

Owner specific advantages for the manufacturing company

This sub-section will include an outline of company C's ownership-specific advantages. Company C's core competencies are within cooling of food, air-conditioning, operation of heat in buildings and speed regulation of el-motors and solutions for sustainable energy, e.g. solar energy. Company C was founded in 1933 and product innovation has ever since been a crucial part of the company's development and growth. 70 years of experience must be assumed to have a significant value to the company and its products. This is reflected in knowledge as well as experience, which are factors that to a great extent are important for the company to protect.

As experience is intangible, it is difficult to detect if it is present. It has to be taken into consideration that company C decided on internalisation as a globalisation strategy and therefore attempted to transfer its knowledge and experience into a subsidiary. Furthermore, the Vice President of company C was relocated to India in order to run the facility and uphold the standards set by the mother company.

The company offers its employees continuing education as well as job related training. During 2008 company C made its global training academy available to more employees via its e-learning platform. In addition the performance within the development of managers has been intensified. The above reflects the company's effort to strengthen the knowledge base internally, which is an important ownership-specific advantage to maintain and protect, seeing the knowledge base as fundamental for product development. This is of great importance to this type of company since the products offered are complex and include a great level of technology.

Compliance is a top priority of company C. This includes risk management being an integrated part of the strategic planning and is carried out through a number of activities, seeking to ensure good cooperation management, good business management, compliance programme, projects, outsourcing, purchasing, insurance, currency, interests, raw materials, reputation, patents, IT systems, contracts, environment etc. As compliance has such great importance and is reflected in so many activities, it can be characterised as an ownership-specific advantage. "Risk Management" is a top driver of the compliance concept. Taken into consideration that ownership-specific advantages involve control, the compliance concept is a unique advantage which company C must protect. If an external business partner was to be included, the company would not be able to monitor if the standards would be adhered to.

In addition to the compliance programme, company C since 2008 had a whistle blower function, where employees anonymously have the opportunity to report possible deviations without any influence from the management. The implementation of compliance was not evident when visiting company C in India. A tour was given around the facility including the manufacturing centre. It was not clarified how for instance the whistle blower function had been implemented in India.

Since 2004 Company C has implemented a code of conduct in respect to its suppliers, stipulating how the suppliers are to act socially and environmentally. In order to check if this is abided, the company performed audits on 22 percent of its suppliers. This is an example of an ownership-specific advantage since it is a concept that strengthens the company's image in relation to corporate responsibility. It also strengthens the overall view of the product's quality, if the customer is ensured that the company upholds a certain standard on environmental issues that could also have a direct effect on the product in terms of for instance the use of certain chemicals during the manufacturing process. During the field studies a subcontractor to company C was visited. A tour around the facility was given including a tour in the manufacturing centre. The code of conduct for company C states that the company:

"... supports the fundamental human right to have sound working conditions. Supplier must ensure a good and safe working environment which complies with all applicable rules and laws. As a minimum:

- *Workers must not be exposed to dangerous work without being properly protected. Workers must be provided personal protection equipment and be instructed in its proper use.*
- *Facilities must provide appropriate light and ventilation*
- *All dangerous materials must be stored in safe places and used in safe and controlled ways.*
- *All machinery must be properly maintained and shielded."*

It was evident that the working conditions at the subcontractor did not comply with the code of conduct. The employees were exposed to dangerous red-hot metal and handled it without any protective working clothes or other safety precautions. The only shield between the employee and the metal was gloves. Furthermore, the manufacturing centre was steaming hot without any other proper ventilation. The machinery was not shielded in a way that could provide protection to the employees.

Owner specific advantages for the knowledge company

Company E has a holistic approach in every aspect of its activities. For instance, the company has a concept called "holistic management" which means that the employees get involved in the making of strategies as well as business plans. This should help ensure commitment, understanding and a feeling that they belong in the company. Another way in which the holistic management approach is used to keep the employees committed is the fact that the employees own about five percent of the company. Furthermore, this holistic view is based on continuous learning and development. The employees get involved at the beginning of the process by helping determine the goals and they stay involved throughout the actions and results in order to identify the areas that need attention. This process keeps repeating itself. In Chennai this holistic perspective was used by giving the employees the opportunity to participate in the projects which they found most interesting. Project boards were displayed in various areas in the department, on which the employees could sign up to participate in a project.

Sustainability is a very high priority within this company. Because of its Nordic roots and the focus on sustainability, it has become a natural step for company E to implement sustainability in both design and projects – this includes CO_2 neutral buildings. This company has also developed a sustainability-tool which generates sustainability into measurable sizes and thereby visualises the degree of sustainability in every aspect of a given project.

However, in Chennai there seems to be no focus on sustainability. The employees spent several hours talking about the company and every aspect they found relevant for us to know. However, sustainability was not mentioned. Therefore, it seems that this owner specific advantage is not as prioritised in Chennai as it is at the mother company.

Their motto *"local partners, global knowledge"* shows a commitment on trying to share knowledge between departments across the world.

The visit at the company in Chennai showed that knowledge sharing forms a large part of the company's identity. To name a few examples, the Chennai department uses tools like Skype, email, video-chat or Lync to communicate with both departments in India and abroad. Furthermore, the company has a data-exchange platform, an intranet and a shared network for document sharing. This applies both globally and nationally. The company experiences that both the mother company and the department in Chennai learn something when focusing on knowledge sharing. Because of the fact that the mother company is situated in a different country, it has been decided to enhance knowledge sharing by sending employees back and forward between the two countries in order to transfer knowledge in the best possible way. It is obvious that the vision on prioritising knowledge sharing from the mother company shines through at the Chennai department.

An overview of the owner specific advantages

After describing the owner specific advantages, Table 5.2 intends to provide some clarification in regards to the two companies.

Table 5.2: Owner specific advantages in Chennai

Company	Owner specific advantages	Implemented in Chennai
Company C	Experience and knowledge	✓
	Continuous education and training for employees	✓
	Compliance	÷
	Code of conduct	÷
Company E	Holistic management	✓
	Sustainability	÷
	Knowledge sharing	✓

Table 5.2 shows that Company C has implemented two out of four owner specific advantages in Chennai, whereas company E has implemented two out of three. According to Dunning it is very important to make sure that the owner specific advantages are not lost, when the company goes global. It therefore raises some questions for the two companies regarding their awareness of the fact, that they did not implement all of their owner specific advantages in Chennai. This can be a deliberate choice for both companies, but it any case the companies must be aware of this.

India as a market for Danish companies

In order to determine the location specific advantages in India the PESTEL analysis will be used in the next section. The PESTEL analysis will be used as an overall model for the Indian market and afterwards the location specific challenges and advantages will be discussed.

Figure 5.2: PESTEL of India

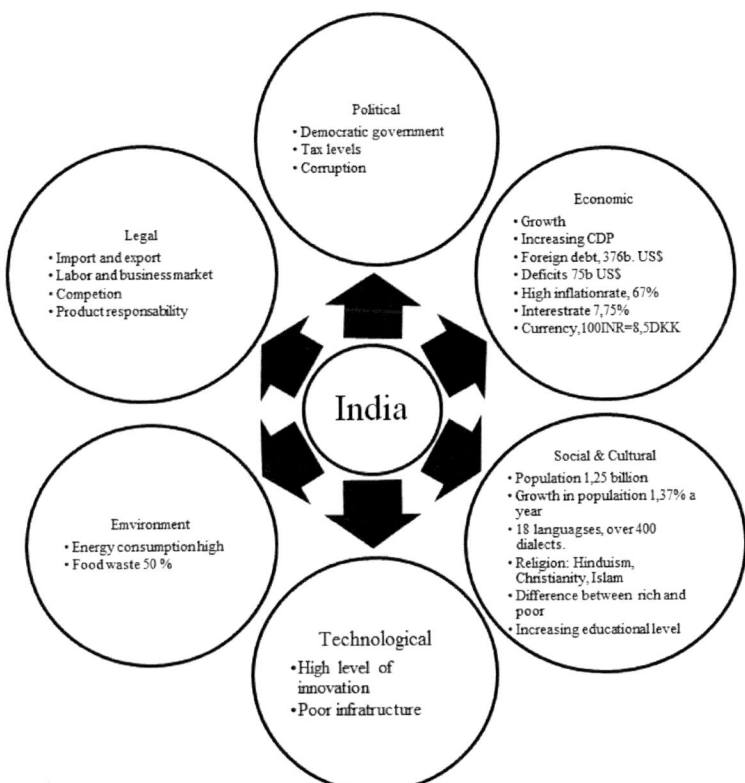

Source: Own elaboration

Political

India is now an independent republic after obtaining independence from the British empire in 1947 (Gosai, 2013).

The political system in India is a democratic government. The parliament consists of two houses: the house of people and the house of state. The house of people consists of 544 directly elected members and the house of state consists of 245 indirectly elected members. For now (end 2013) the president is Mr. Shri Pranab Mukherjee. He has been in office since July 25th 2012 and he is from the Indian National Congress party. The president works on advice from his prime-minister and the cabinet. The role of the president is mostly ceremonial, and therefore the political power realistically lies with the prime-minster, Dr. Manmohan Singh from the National Congress Party. The next election is scheduled to take place in 2014. The biggest challenge for the government is the economic reforms.

The focus is to improve the living conditions of a larger part of the population. Furthermore, it is a priority to strengthen the economic growth at a time with limited international economic growth because of the financial crisis (Udenrigsministeriet, 2013).

According to several companies the political situation in India could have been better. The CEO of company C explained that legislation procedures in India are very difficult to follow because of the way in which India is organised. There are 18 states, and the legislation kicks in at different times in each state. Furthermore, it was mentioned that in Denmark the government has about two years between elections to launch reforms, and this is not the case in India. Moreover, this CEO (company C) finds that the political parties seem to know how to create a better business environment, but they just refuse to do so. Company A explained that the two big parties have similar economic policies, but they still insist on shooting down each other's ideas instead of making compromises (Company A).

Corruption is a huge challenge in India. According to the transparency corruption index, India is number 94 out of 175 countries (Transparency international, 2013).

According to company A, the tax system in India is quite confusing and it properly would be helpful for foreign companies in India to seek some guidance on the subject (Company A). There is a difference in the tax level depending on the company being local or foreign. For domestic companies the tax rate is about 30 percent and for foreign companies it is about 40 percent (World Wide Tax, 2013).

Economics

India's economy has grown by six to ten percent over the last ten years which makes it one of the world's fastest growing economies as well as the 4th largest economy (Undervisningsministeriet, 2013).

India has changed from being an impoverished country to being an emerging global economy. The economic growth is divided into two phases, namely the first 45 years after the independence and the last 20 years as a free market economy. During the first phase India's economy was divided into two segments – the public and the private sector. The private sector owned small to medium sized businesses and industries which were protected by the government. The purpose of the large extension of government operations was to provide services at a reasonable cost but progress was limited due to India's democratic system. The reason for

India's slow progress in economic development during the first 45 years was among other things that the country had no focus on economic improvement and therefore economic policies were non-existent. After the collapse of the Soviet Union, the Indian economy was impacted significantly seeing that The Soviet Union was India's major trade partner. The International Monetary Fund (MF) and the World Bank offered help to India in exchange for economic reforms in 1991. The reforms also included an opening for foreign countries in order to boost the economy (Company A). Before the reforms FDI was restricted to 40 percent. This barrier was removed and led multinational companies to increase their stake levels resulting in a significant increase in FDI's in just three years. Tariff levels were also lowered, the exchange rate policy was reformed and industrialised licensing policy was liberalised.

The main drivers of the economic growth can mainly be attributed to the increase in FDI's, India's expertise in information technology and increased domestic consumption because of a growing middle class population. India's GDP per capita is 3,662 USD in 2013 (Udenrigsministeriet, 2013).

According to the statistical profile of India by OECD, the growth in GDP per capita has been relatively significant during a period of eight years. In 2005 the GDP per capita was 2,276 USD (OECD, 2013). The real GDP growth is 5-0 percent (Udenrigsministeriet, 2013).

India has a foreign debt of 376.3 billion USD and has a deficit of 75 billion USD in the balance of trade (OECD, 2013). The currency of India is Indian rupees and 100 INR is equivalent to 8.50 DKK. The inflation rate was according to tradingeconomics.com 7.5 percent in November 2013 (Fontes, 2013). The increase has been significant compared to 10 years ago in 2003 where the inflation rate was 3.72 percent. It is an increase of approximately 100 percent. According to company A the inflation rate today is approximately 67 percent (Company A).

The interest rate has recently been increased by India's central bank to 7.75 percent. The reason is that the inflation is likely to remain elevated (Reuters, 2013). The interest rate has increased by approximately two percent over the last ten years. The increase is attributed to the high inflation.

The lower wages in India are of great interest for foreign companies when considering FDI's as well as outsourcing. India has a minimum wage of 0.28 USD (Boesler, 2013). According to company A, the wage levels in India are really low compared to other countries, and it is believed that most foreign companies are especially attracted by this factor (Company A).

Social and cultural

India has a population of more than 1.25 billion people, with an annual growth of 1.37 percent. The most widespread religions are Hinduism, Islam and Christianity. There are 18 official languages, where Hindu and English are the main languages. However, it is possible to do business in English (Company A).The educational level has been increasing over the last years. Specifically India is focused on the engineering education (Company A). In Southern India there are 16 engineering universities, and every year 160,000 engineering students' graduate. The company also mentioned that Bangalore in Southern India is a hub for engineers (Company A). The increasing educational level combined with FDI, which was described in the economical part, contributed to the economic growth in India and is therefore important for the government to keep focusing on.

Technological

The expertise in ICT and the improved protection of intellectual property have made many Western firms move their R&D departments to India (Gosai, 2013). The infrastructure in India is the biggest supply chain challenge according to Rick Blasgen, President and CEO, Council of Supply Chain Management Professionals (Law, 2013). The poor infrastructure is causing bottlenecks physically resulting in goods not being able to make the destination in time. After having experienced the infrastructure in Chennai, India first hand, the problems are evident. Traffic jams are a rule rather than an exception and cause a lot of waiting on the road. Rick Blasgen argues that if the infrastructure was to be improved to enable products to reach the villages, it would result in possible new markets. According to Blasgen India has the potential to become a supply chain centre of excellence for the world (Law, 2013).

Environmental

Due to the growth of GDP in India, there is an even greater demand for the country's energy resources. At this time, 54 percent of the electricity generation capacity is based on coal, whereas other renewables like wind, solar and sun only count for two percent. Furthermore, it is noted that the power-grid is quite unstable (Ministry of statistics and programmes implementation, 2013). The CEO of company C explained that sometimes the power goes out, and then the emergency generators kick in. This also happened during our visit at the company.

Food waste is a huge challenge in India. The CEO of company C explained that there is up to 50 percent food wasted. This food waste is quite interesting when you take into consideration that the inflation food-rate has increased (Reuters, 2013).

Challenges and advantages in India

The following sections will describe the challenges and advantages of outsourcing or offshoring to India. The issues are selected as a result of the importance of these expressed by the companies visited in Chennai. Both the international companies as well as the Indian companies explained how several of the issues listed in the following section influence the pros and cons of locating in India. Furthermore the points are supported by extractions from the PESTEL analysis as well as by own experiences.

Location challenges

The political system in India works in some ways like most other democratic states. The challenge in India is that the country is divided in 18 different states. The rules and regulations of the country may not apply at the same time in every state (Company C), which makes it difficult for companies to coordinate their activities in case these are located in different states. It is assumed that this challenge applies for both manufacturing and knowledge companies, since both depend on rules and regulations being as easy as possible to comprehend.

The corruption could also present a problem for companies trying to do business in India. In countries where the systems are not transparent it creates uncertainty about the way you are treated. Many of the companies in India expressed that trust was a crucial part of cooperation (Company Z). India's low score in the corruption perceptions index is a barrier that can create uncertainty with the foreign companies. Furthermore, another company mentioned transparency as an important factor as well in order to achieve a valuable partnership (Company Y). It is interesting to point out that Indians see transparency as an important element, taken into consideration that corruption is very common in India. This challenge applies for both production and knowledge companies.

As explained earlier in this chapter, the taxes in India are quite high (40 percent) Furthermore, it is difficult to figure out how the tax system works and it would be a good idea to approach a consulting company in order to get some help to understand the rules (Company A). However the corporate taxes depend on the income of the company. The more you earn the higher percentage tax you have to pay. This goes for both manufacturing and knowledge companies, and it is therefore the belief that this location specific challenge applies for both types of companies. However, this could become a significant challenge if the companies' size (in turnover) is taken into consideration.

The infrastructure in Chennai and in India in general is quite poor. Chennai has about 10,000,000 citizens, and the roads are badly constructed and almost all transportation is done by cars, scooters etc. In Chennai they are at this moment occupied by constructing a metro-system which will lift a burden from the regular traffic once it is done. However, several of the foreign companies believe that this metro-project will take quite a long time. This is mostly because of the fact that in general the Indians do not see time in the same perspective as the Western societies. Therefore they are not used to having to finish a project by a specific deadline. Even if a deadline is stated, they do not mind if it is exceeded (Company C).

It is the belief that the infrastructure represents a bigger problem for the manufacturing companies than for the knowledge companies in relation to transportation of products. At company F it was explained that a shipment was supposed to leave Chennai on a Thursday. However, the shipment was not on route before the following Monday. Being a foreign company used to an infrastructure without any huge difficulties, you have to be aware of this. A workaround on this problem could be to have the shipments ready some time ahead of the deadline in order to get the products to the end customers in time. For knowledge companies, the challenge is getting the employees back and forth between their homes and their workplace. Company D has implemented a system by which the employees are picked up and taken to the company, and at the end of the day they are taken back home. This ensures that the employees have the possibility to be at the company on time.

The power grid is quite unstable in Chennai. Most companies invest in an emergency generator in case of the power grid failing (Company C). However, this location specific challenge is relatively small compared to other problems, but it is still vital for the companies to know in order to be prepared for the power to fail once in a while. This challenge can be of great importance for some manufacturing companies. The production can be extremely dependent on constant power. There is a risk that a batch might be ruined if power failure occurs, even only for a few seconds. If the machinery is not programmed to start up by itself again even though the generator kicks in immediately, the company is dependent on having manpower at the plant around the clock. This is also a challenge for knowledge companies as well as a challenge if computers start shutting down and crucial work might be lost.

A long-term location specific challenge is the energy resources. For now most resources used in India are natural resources. However, these will not last forever, and taking into consideration that India is not yet 100 percent focused on switching to more alternative options like solar and wind power, it might represent a problem in the long run. This is a greater risk and problem for the manufacturing companies, since their demands for energy resources may be assumed to be relatively large. Natural resources do not play as important a role for knowledge companies, seeing their products are intangible in the form of services.

Location-specific advantages

India has experienced a considerable economic growth during the last ten years. As mentioned in the PESTEL analysis, India's economy has grown by six to ten percent which makes it one of the world's fastest growing economies. This fact has made India an attractive market for foreign companies. The increase in domestic consumption because of a growing middle class population also gives manufacturing companies producing luxury goods the opportunity to exploit the market. This is also reflected in the inflation rate, which reflects an increase in consumption. The economic growth is a great location specific advantage for both knowledge companies as well as manufacturing companies. Seeing the consumption is increasing, it creates a bigger demand, and the supply has to follow in order to uphold growth. Manufacturing companies can benefit from the opportunity by penetrating an entire new market, and knowledge companies can benefit from the growth by for instance helping manufacturing companies implement systems that will help optimise end expand their production.

In addition there is also a drawback to the economic growth in the long run. What is currently a location specific advantage can evolve into being a location specific challenge. Seeing an economy is growing, several factors will follow and this could include labour costs. Even though labour costs operate as an advantage at this point, it might not be in ten years.

India is a huge country with over 1 billion citizens. The extent of the population makes India a huge and attractive market for pretty much every product you might be selling. Furthermore it ensures that the companies have many choices for employees since there is no lack of manpower. This will be a benefit for both knowledge and manufacturing companies.

The main language in India is English which also works as a huge location specific advantage. Everyone understands and speaks English which makes it easy to do business and negotiate with local suppliers (Company A). One company compared India to China and it was stated, that even though China is a huge market it is much easier to run a business in India because the language barrier is practically non-existent (Company C). This will apply for both knowledge and manufacturing companies seeing that both have to be able to communicate with their employees, partners, suppliers etc.

The higher level of education is an important location specific advantage. For knowledge companies it is an advantage because they will find qualified workers in India and thereby save resources in relation to recruiting qualified employees for their subsidiary. Manufacturing companies benefit from the higher education level as well in terms of for instance qualified R&D departments which are of great importance especially regarding highly technological products. Since India has a higher level of education and the rate of highly educated engineers is increasing, it also offers opportunities for alternative globalisation strategies. If offshoring has been used because of uncertainties revolving the quality of the output, it opens up the opportunity for using outsourcing as a globalisation strategy instead. Furthermore, it is beneficial for both types of companies hence the manufacturing companies are able to optimise their processes by using for instance advanced IT-solutions developed by knowledge companies.

During the economic reforms India established some years ago, the protection of intellectual property was improved. Both manufacturing and knowledge companies benefit from this. It may also result in companies choosing outsourcing because the fear of not having control of a process, which could be closely connected with one of its ownership-specific advantages, would be minimised. This is not a given thing, but a possibility.

On a short-term basis the natural resources could present an advantage. Most Western companies are used to always having to "think green". Green solutions are most often more expensive for companies to implement. Furthermore, regulations made by the government in several countries and especially in Denmark cause companies to be forced into implement these solutions. Due to the presence of natural resources in India this may attract foreign companies. In this way the companies would not be assigned to green solutions.

A huge location specific advantage in relation to entering the Indian market is low wages. As mentioned earlier the wages are some of the lowest in the world and this is a huge driver for companies to choose to relocate some or all of their activities because of the great impact wages have on cost minimisation, which most companies focus constantly on. As time has gone by and the Indians get more educated, not only the wages of blue collar workers attract companies but also white collar wages. The foreign companies in Chennai are impressed by the expertise and knowhow of the employees (Company F). One company asked a rhetorical question: *"Why employ one engineer in Denmark, when I can have four just as good engineers in Chennai, for the same money?"* (Company C). In addition it is a well-known fact that COOP in Denmark moved an entire accounting division to India in order to minimise costs (Okkels, 2013).

A location specific advantage, which is not included in the PESTEL analysis, is the fact that Chennai is a" hub" for Danish companies. There is a particular street, named "Danish street", in which several Danish companies are located. This could be an advantage in the sense that both knowledge companies and production companies can benefit from each other by comparing and exchanging experience on the Indian market, business style, business traditions etc. (Company A).

Furthermore it is important to underline that these advantages apply not only for the two cases examined or for the other seven companies. It also applies for the companies' competitors as well. As discussed some of the advantages may vary in importance, dependent on which type of company it concerned.

Choosing a globalisation strategy

After having discussed both companies' owner-specific advantages and compared knowledge companies' and manufacturing companies' location specific advantages and challenges, this section will include a reflection on whether internalisation has been the optimal choice for the two case studies and if there are factors that could affect the choice of a globalisation strategy in another direction.

A term mentioned by nearly all the companies was trust and the importance of its presence. It seems as though the trust issue both implied the Indian business partners as well as the foreign business partners. The reason for trust being in the centre of attention could be that India and Western companies have extremely different cultures regarding not only the social aspect but also the business aspect. Indian companies have a high level of hierarchy, whereas Western companies have a very flat structure (Company E). It may be difficult for an Indian employee to trust for instance a Danish if the person does not exude authority, and it may be difficult for a Danish employee to trust an Indian that exudes authority to such extent that the Dane does not feel a dialogue is possible. Furthermore, company E perceived Danes as being very direct in their way of expressing themselves, whereas Indians are very indirect. This could result in several misunderstandings which can cause trust issues. This could be the reason for companies being inclined to use internalisation as a globalisation strategy. In addition, the fact that India is an emerging economy also has to be considered. Since the inflow of foreign companies is still increasing, the market is not stable in the sense that India is still unknown territory for many foreign companies which creates uncertainties and scepticism.

It was evident that in India network was important in relation to surviving as a foreign company (Company B). As a consequence of the lack of network it is difficult for foreign companies to establish a key position in the market. It can be argued that by using externalisation as a globalisation strategy it would be easier to build a network before making an FDI. According to company B it can take up to three years to build up a trustful partnership. Seeing an FDI is much more expensive and the risks are many it can be argued that because of difficulties in building partnerships it could be beneficial to outsource or source activities and subsequently convert the strategy into internalisation.

In addition to the above-mentioned, another globalisation strategy opportunity could be that of joint ventures. In order to accommodate the issues revolving both trust and network a joint venture would be an evident opportunity. According to company X long-term relationships are of great importance. A joint venture is an open opportunity to penetrate the market as a foreign company and to establish a stable network. It is also more economical for the company to contract a joint venture agreement than establishing a fully owned subsidiary. Furthermore the opportunity for future acquisition exists if the intention is to gain full control. Moreover the foreign company is still able to maintain control in respect to its ownership specific advantages by using joint venture as a globalisation strategy.

If the two case companies C and E are to be assessed as to whether they have chosen the most suitable strategy to enter the Indian market, it can be concluded that internalisation has turned out to be a profitable strategy. They have been able to protect and maintain control of their ownership specific advantages and have penetrated the Indian market successfully. It is important to emphasise that both cases are part of big international concerns which are assumed to have a great extent of capital. If risks are taken into consideration, the economic risks related to internalisation may not appear as being of as great importance as would be the case if the company was smaller. Furthermore it is likely that a large concern has a more stable and established network. This is not necessarily located in India but it might have the effect that authority status is easier accomplished compared to a smaller company. A joint venture might be a better choice for a smaller company in order to state its existence by cooperating with local partners. In conclusion it can be argued that the size of the company reflected in turnover as well as actual size could influence the success of the chosen globalisation strategy.

India is a country of opportunities for foreign companies to explore. The difficulties and challenges in establishing not only a position but a key position in the Indian market are many and are yet to overcome. Despite this it seems that India as well as the foreign companies are moving towards an acceptance and tolerance in terms of one another's existence. India is still an upcoming economy but by the help of FDI's, foreign inputs and its own expertise, it has the potential of becoming one of the world's largest economies.

Resume

The theme of this chapter is an overall discussion of outsourcing vs. offshoring when entering the Indian market and whether there is a difference depending on the company being a manufacturing or a knowledge company. Two companies have been selected as illustrative cases.

In order to examine this subject Dunning's eclectic paradigm with elaboration by Teit Lüthje was used. This framework consists of owner specific advantages, location specific advantages and the choice of globalisation strategy which can be either externalisation or internalisation. It is found that both companies has several owner specific advantages, however, not all of them are implemented in Chennai. This can, however, be a deliberate choice from the companies' perspective.

Hereafter a PESTEL analysis was used in order to identify the location specific advantages. To name a few it was found that low wages, increase in educational level and the economic growth are location specific advantages, whereas infrastructure, corruption and high corporate taxes are location specific challenges. After discussing these advantages and challenges it is found that there is a slight difference depending on it being a manufacturing company or a knowledge company. For instance, the infrastructure challenge might be a bigger problem for manufacturing companies because they have to consider delivery of the physical products they produce.

Finally it was discussed whether or not the two companies have chosen the right globalisation strategy. With the findings in this chapter it is the writer's belief that the two companies are well established and therefore it cannot be a wrong decision for them having used internalisation. However, after visiting the many companies and understanding more of the Indian culture it has come to the writer's attention that a third option might be present in order to enter the Indian market, i.e. using joint venture as a globalisation strategy.

OLIE model – the right way to go?

The OLIE-model is an overall framework which sheds light on factors that could be of importance for companies to consider before deciding upon a globalisation strategy. The OLIE-model is not a clear-cut theoretical basis for companies to use, but it is an appropriate starting point and creates room for adjustments and additions of various theories that might be applicable to the individual companies. Furthermore, as mentioned, other strategies could be applied in order to extend the model hence it covers more solutions than just internalisation and externalisation. This could for instance include joint venture.

Conclusion

After having discussed both companies' owner specific advantages and compared knowledge companies' and manufacturing companies' location specific advantages and challenges, this section will include a reflection on whether internalisation has been the optimal choice for the two case studies and if there are factors that could affect the choice of a globalisation strategy in another direction.

A term mentioned by nearly all the companies was trust and the importance of its presence. It seems as though the trust issue applied for the Indian business partners as well as the foreign business partners. The reason for trust being in the centre of attention could be that Indian and Western companies have extremely different cultures regarding not only the social aspect but also the business aspect. Indian companies have a high level of hierarchy, whereas Western companies have a very flat structure (Company E). It may be difficult for an Indian to trust a Danish employee if the person does not exude authority and it may be difficult for a Danish employee to trust an Indian that exudes authority to such an extent that the Dane does not feel a dialogue is possible. Furthermore company E perceived Danes as being very direct in their way of expressing themselves, whereas Indians are very indirect. This could result in several misunderstandings which can cause trust issues. This could be the reason for companies being inclined to use internalisation as a globalisation strategy. In addition, the fact that India is an emerging economy also has to be countered in. Since the inflow of foreign companies is still increasing, the market is not stable in the sense that India is still unknown territory for many foreign companies which creates uncertainties and scepticism.

It was evident that in India network was important in relation to surviving as a foreign company (Company B). As a consequence of the lack of network it is difficult for foreign companies to establish a key position in the market. It can be argued that by using externalisation as a globalisation strategy it would be easier to build up a network before making a FDI. Company B states it may take up to three years to build a trustful partnership. Seeing that a FDI is much more expensive and the risks are many, it is arguable that due to difficulties in building partnerships it could be beneficial to outsource activities and subsequently convert the strategy into internalisation.

In addition to the above-mentioned, another globalisation strategy opportunity could be a joint venture. In order to accommodate the issues revolving both trust and network, a joint venture would be an evident opportunity. According to company X long-term relationships are of great importance. A joint venture is an open opportunity both to penetrate the market as a foreign company and also to establish a stable network. It is also more economical for the company to contract a joint venture agreement than establishing a fully owned subsidiary. Furthermore the opportunity for future acquisition exists if the intention is to gain full control. Moreover the foreign company is still able to maintain control in respect to its ownership specific advantages by using joint venture as a globalisation strategy.

If the two case companies C and E are to be assessed in terms whether they have chosen the most suitable strategy to enter the Indian market, it can be concluded that internalisation has turned out to be a profitable strategy. They have been able to protect and maintain control of their ownership specific advantages and have penetrated the Indian market successfully. It is important to emphasize that both companies are part of larger companies, which are assumed to have a great amount of capital. If risks are taken into consideration, the economic risks related to internalisation may not appear of just as great importance as it would if the company was smaller. Furthermore it is likely that a larger concern has a more stable and established network. This is not necessarily located in India but it might have the effect that authority status is easier accomplished compared to a smaller company. Joint venture might be a better choice for a smaller company in order to state its existence by cooperating with local partners. In conclusion it can be argued that the size of the company reflected in both turnover as well as actual size could influence the success of the chosen globalisation strategy.

India is a country of opportunities for foreign companies to explore. The difficulties and challenges by establishing not only a position but a key position in the Indian market are many and are yet to overcome. Despite the above-mentioned it seems that India as well as the foreign companies are moving towards an acceptance and tolerance towards one another's existence. India is still an upcoming economy but by the help of FDI's, foreign inputs and its own expertise, it has the potential of becoming one of the world's largest economies.

CHAPTER 6

Epilogue: Learning and Reflection

Ole Stegmann Mikkelsen, Jan Stentoft & Antony Paulraj

Abstract

The aim of this chapter is to summarise and conclude on the process, the results, and the technical as well as social learning elements for the students. The chapter is based on an evaluating questionnaire survey answered by the students. The chapter ends with extracting the overall conclusions for the four themes of the field study trip.

Introduction

This chapter is a reflection on the course *International Field Studies* offered by the Department of Entrepreneurship and Relationship Management at the University of Southern Denmark in Kolding. The objective of the course is in the course description stated as:

> '*The aim of International Field Studies is to develop the students' skills in applying specific theories and approaches from a general ontological, epistemological, and methodological perspective to a concrete business problem in a problem driven collaboration with other students. Furthermore, the purpose is also for the students to obtain experience with the necessary technical, social, and ethical competencies required in conducting international field work.*"

Hence, the aim of the course is to develop the students' skills in conducting all phases of a smaller field study. This includes preparatory desk research, organisation of the field work, and the completion of subsequent analyses and writing up reports.

To follow up on the above mentioned purpose of the course the students were asked to fill in a brief online questionnaire after returning home from India. The questionnaire included eight questions. Three were open ended questions allowing the students to reflect and comment on their own experience and learning. The rest of the questions were answered on a 7-point Likert scale (1 = low degree of agreement and 7 = high degree). All 16 enrolled students answered the eight questions. The results of this survey are presented here as it is believed they can provide learning to others outside the department in which the course is offered. The results may for example be of interest to others in the process of planning or executing similar courses. Furthermore, the structure of the course puts the students in physical proximity to the core content of the theoretical studies, why it contributes to the continuous discussion on creating stimulating learning environments, also in courses of longer duration.

The chapter is further on organised in short sections in which the students' feedback on the most impressive experiences during the field trip is presented. The chapter ends by presenting conclusions on the overall study trip and a brief conclusion on the respective student chapters' findings.

Most impressive experiences

Firstly, the students were asked to reflect on and rank what they perceive as the three most impressive experiences during the field study trip. The results are:

1. Experiencing the difference in Indian culture compared to Danish culture
2. The company visits. Visiting both Danish and Indian companies gave a better understanding of business culture and culture in a broader sense
3. The social aspect of traveling with fellow students

Likewise the students were asked to evaluate whether the course gave them a better understanding of relevant theories to address and solve their research questions. The results of this question are shown in Figure 6.1.

Figure 6.1: Better understanding of relevant theories and methods

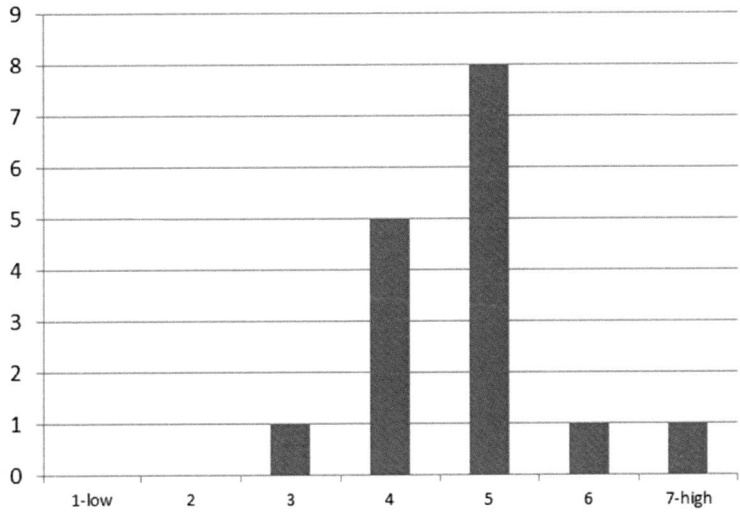

The average score is 4.75 on the seven point scale. With the average and the distribution illustrated in Figure 6.1, the students indicate that to some degree they have obtained a better understanding of relevant theories and methods during the course. Thus, working closely with the subject matter in India has provided the students with new understandings of theories and methods learned in Denmark, and they have learned how to adjust these to other contexts. Hence, students should not only learn the relevant theories, but must also understand the limitations of the theories and how to apply them in practice.

Application of relevant theories and methods

The students were likewise asked to evaluate the degree to which they felt challenged in using relevant theories and methods in order to address and solve their research questions formulated in their respective assignments. The result is illustrated in Figure 6.2.

Figure 6.2: Application of relevant theories and methods

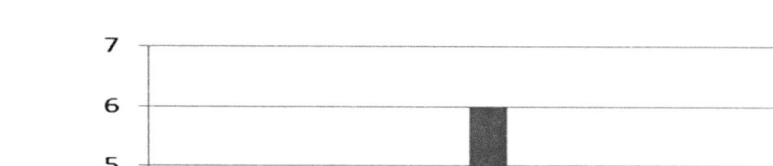

The result in Figure 6.2 suggests that the students feel they have been challenged in finding relevant theories to be used to address and cover the research questions in their respective assignments (se chapter 2 to 5). The average is 4.94 on a seven point scale. Before the field study trip the group found themselves to be relatively confident with their theory selection. However, their stay in India with the interviews, observations and personal presence in the Indian culture provided them with a more nuanced view of relevant theories and methods and how to apply them.

Improved competencies through group work

The students were then asked to evaluate if participation in the course had improved their competencies (in conducting group work). The results to this question are shown in Figure 6.3.

Figure 6.3: Improved social competencies through group work

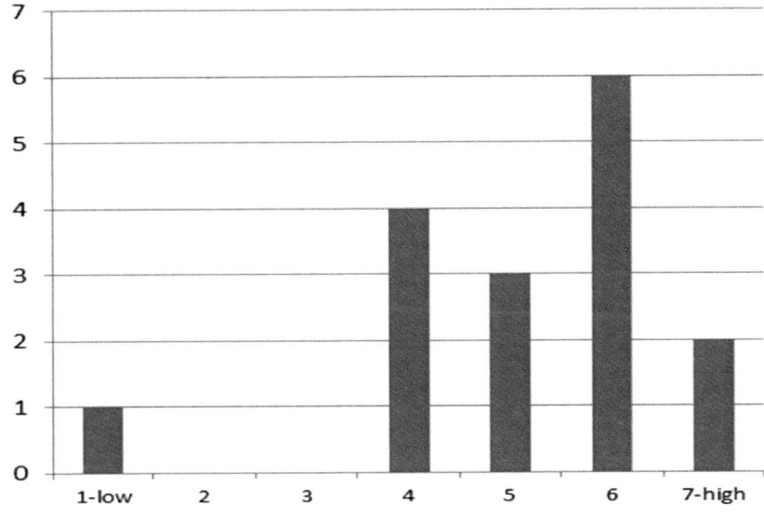

From the answers, and with an average score on 5.13, it appears that most students perceive that they have improved their social competencies with respect to group work from a medium to a high degree. At the time of the evaluation the students have returned to Denmark and were still in the process of writing up their assignments. Up to this point they have mainly been working with the theories and methodologies for their assignment, and data analysis had just begun. Not all groups organised the work in the same way. Some groups worked very closely together in all aspects of the assignment, while other groups divided the work into sub-groups with specific responsibilities.

Better understanding of Indian culture

The students were also asked to reflect upon whether the field study trip provided them with a better understanding of Indian culture. The results are illustrated in Figure 6.4.

Figure 6.4: Better understanding of Indian culture

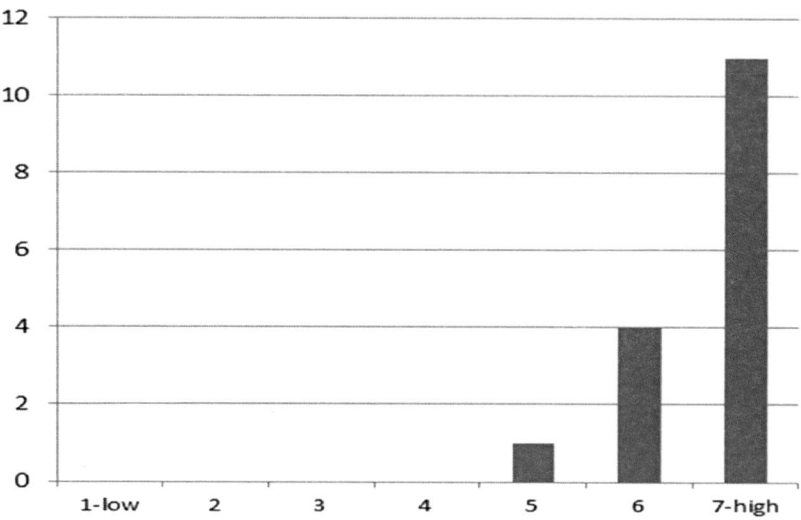

The distribution illustrated in Figure 6.4 with an average score on 6.63 gives a significant indication that the field study trip has provided the students with a deeper insight into the Indian culture and society. The overall programme was comprehensive and packed with many company visits. The visited companies included cultural aspects of doing business in India in their presentations and discussions. This provided the students with valuable first and second hand insights from people actually living in the culture. Together with actually being in the city of Chennai, this has provided them much cultural learning and understanding.

The most important points of cultural learning

Finally, the students were asked what they perceived to be the most giving cultural learning from the field study trip. The question was open ended. The elements most often mentioned are summarised below.

- The immense contrast between rich and poor
- The eagerness of Indian companies to learn, and how far they are
- The avoidance of saying "no" - "yes" is not always a "yes"
- The caste system, also in companies
- Culture is not just culture. Companies have very different cultures

Conclusion

This book is entitled *Doing Business in India: Selected Themes to Consider*. More than ever companies are doing business across borders, and the global economy is becoming more complex through global sourcing and trade from all over the world. The students have chosen the themes because of their practical relevance for the time being. Many Western companies have discussed the potential of India. Not only as a destination for low cost country (LCC) sourcing, but more and more also in terms of location for production and in terms of an emerging market with its high population. Therefore, offshoring and localisation strategies were considered as central themes to investigate during the field study trip. Due to the increased activity with Indian companies and society, Indian culture and business culture were likewise considered important for the study. From a manufacturing perspective India has been perceived as a low skilled "arm's and leg's" production site. However, India is rapidly moving away from a pure low-cost country profile to a high-value country in terms of innovative products. At the same time India is one of the major destinations for IT outsourcing/offshoring. Therefore both innovation and knowledge management were included as themes. Conclusions on the questions of each of the four themes are briefly provided in the following.

Indian business culture

When engaging in business in foreign countries it is important to pay attention to cultural aspects. This is also true when doing business in India. To succeed one must pay attention and adapt to local customs, habits and traditions. Danish companies face a number of challenges when doing business in India. In the chapter on Indian business culture the following questions guided the research:

1. *How do Indian employees react in regard to formal hierarchy structure within the company?*
2. *To which degree is the Indian society collectivistic or individualistic?*
3. *In what way does the Indian society control uncertainty regarding the future?*
4. *Which values define the Indian society?*
5. *To what degree does time matter in the Indian society?*

Traditionally one would think that Indian businesses are very hierarchical. This is to a large degree true, but the study also showed that the Western companies are less hierarchical, while domestic companies with little

Western interaction are more hierarchical. Although India has moved towards a more global orientation, the higher level of hierarchy means that employees do not express themselves as openly and direct as in Western companies. This makes the ability to provide direction and exercise control an important requirement in India. As a collectivistic country, compared to Denmark, relationships and team decision-making are very important issues in India. In a Western context exchange and transactions are most important, followed by relationships, while in an Indian context relationships are more important. The ability to create network and trustful personal and social relationships is important in order to do business in India.

Innovation in India

The chapter on innovation provides an overall knowledge of the way in which Indian companies work with innovation, and adds an increased understanding of innovation in an Indian context. To pursue this, the following research questions were formulated:

1. *What are the current drivers of innovation in India?*
2. *In which areas do Danish and Indian companies innovate in India?*
3. *What other factors should Danish and Indian companies be aware of regarding innovation?*

The analysis identified an increased political and governmental focus on innovation through focused campaigns, designated innovation councils and legislation promoting cross-national cooperation. The huge number of highly skilled and low-cost engineers graduating every year likewise impacts the product development knowledge foundation.

All four innovation types – product, process, position and paradigm innovation - were found in the analysis of the companies. Process innovation was found to be most common, indicating a focus on cost and quality. India still struggles with high inflation. Other challenges for the innovation drivers are the political system, which is still bureaucratic, and the corruption. However, changes are initiated.

Knowledge Management

The aim of this chapter is to investigate and discuss how a company can ensure that knowledge is nurtured so that it flows throughout the company, available to all involved parties. The chapter raises two questions:

1. *What kind of knowledge management strategy should be used, when offshoring or outsourcing to India?*
2. *Which focus areas are important when transferring knowledge to your partner in India?*

It is important to acknowledge and consider the cultural differences when pursuing Knowledge Management. Unlike the Danish culture, in which it is common to give feedback no matter what status one has in the hierarchy, Indians do not have the same mind-set. The empirical research revealed five important aspects to consider to achieve effective Knowledge Management. These are: building trust, continuous training of Indian employees, understanding the difference in managerial styles, developing a long term relationship and achieving organisational transparency through data sharing. Some companies built digital platforms to share knowledge, while others leaned more to 'cultural ambassadors'. Findings show that human relations are important in an Indian company, for which reason a strategy with the right expats can be an important lever for success with Knowledge Management in an Indian context.

Outsourcing or offshoring?

The aim of this chapter is to investigate the main challenges of the two globalisation strategies offshoring and outsourcing to India and to understand the learning hereof. This is based on two case companies; one manufacturing and one knowledge company. The aim is to answer the following questions:

1. *What are the two cases' owner specific advantages*
   a. *How do they ensure that these are maintained in their departments in Chennai?*
2. *What challenges do companies face when doing business in India?*
   a. *Is there a difference depending on the company being a manufacturing company or a knowledge company?*
3. *Is it appropriate for the two cases to have chosen an internalisation strategy with regard to the Indian market?*

Based on a literature review and interviews with the visited companies, globalisation strategies of externalisation or internalisation are discussed.

The OLIE model is used as framework for the discussion. The framework consists of <u>o</u>wner specific advantages, <u>l</u>ocation specific advantages and the choice of the globalisation strategy <u>e</u>xternalisation or <u>i</u>nternalisation. Both companies hold ownership advantages, off which however, not all are implemented in the Chennai branch. Advantages are found to be the low cost, increasing educational level and economic growth, while the challenges faced are infrastructure, corruption and high corporate taxes. The challenges are somewhat different if the company is a manufacturing or a knowledge based company. Most obviously is the physical infrastructure more challenging for a manufacturing company as it needs physically components to be transported to and from the company premises.

List of References

Abernathy, W.J. and Clark, K.B. (1985), "Innovation: Mapping the winds of creative destruction", *Research Policy*, Vol. 14, No. 1, pp. 3-22.

Alavi, M. and Leidner, D.E. (2001), "Knowledge Management and Knowledge Management Systems: Conceptual Foundations and Research Issues", *MIS Quarterly*, Vol. 25, No. 1, pp. 107-136.

Ambos, T.C. and Ambos, B. (2009), "The Impact of distance on knowledge transfer effectiveness in multinational corporations", *Journal of International Management*, Vol. 15, No. 1, pp.1-14.

AP Reporter (2013), "How Gillette execs spent a fortune developing a razor for India using MIT student focus groups...without considering the country's lack of running water", available at: http://www.dailymail.co.uk/news/article-2443191/Gillette-spent-fortune-Indian-razor-forgetting-countrys-running-water.html, accessed 17th November, 2013.

Arlbjørn, J.S., Lüthje, T., Mikkelsen, O.S., Schlichter, Jakob and Thoms, L. (2013): *Danske producenters udflytning og hjemtagning af produktion*, Kraks Fond Byforskning, København.

Boesler, M. (2013), "Here's How America's Minimum Wage Stacks Up Against Countries Like India, Russia, Greece, and France", available at: http://www.businessinsider.com/a-look-at-minimum-wages-around-the-world-2013-8#ixzz2nw9oUrVH, accessed 7th December, 2013.

Boisot, M.H. (2010): *Knowledge Assets: Securing Competitive Advantage in the Information Economy*, Oxford University Press, New York.

Boughzala, I. and Briggs, R.O. (2012), "A value frequency model of knowledge sharing: an exploratory study on knowledge sharability in cross-organizational collaboration", *Electron Markets*, pp. 9-19.

Business Standard, 2014. Tamil Nadu attracts FDI faster, says study. http://www.business-standard.com/article/economy-policy/tamil-nadu-attracts-fdi-faster-says-study-112071202025_1.html, accessed on September 01, 2014.

Carlsen, M. and Jensen, A.M. (2008), "Globalisering og danske direkte Investeringer", available at: https://www.nationalbanken.dk/C1256BE2005737D3/side/Globaliseri

ng og danske direkte investeringer/$file/KVO_08_kap4.pdf, accessed 12th December 2013.

Chang, Y., Gong, Y. and Peng, M.W. (2012), : "Expatriate knowledge transfer, subsidiary absorptive capacity, and subsidiary performance", *Academy of Management Journal*, Vol. 55, No. 4, pp. 927-948.

Chataway, J., Hanlin, R. and Kaplinsky, R. (2013), "Inclusive Innovation: An Architecture for Policy Development", available at: https://www.sussex.ac.uk/webteam/gateway/file.php?name=kaplinsky-chataway-hanlin-framing-policy-for-inclusive-innovation-ikd-dp.pdf&site=25, accessed 18th November, 2013.

Chaturvedi, A. and Sachitanand, R. (2013), "A million engineers in India struggling to get placed in an extremely challenging market", available at: http://articles.economictimes.indiatimes.com/2013-06-18/news/40049243_1_engineers-iit-bombay-batch-size, accessed 18th November, 2013.

Choudhury, S.D. and Munroe, T. (2013), "India raises interest rates again, warns on stubborn inflation", available at: http://www.reuters.com/article/2013/10/29/us-india-economy-cbank-idUSBRE99S05V20131029, accessed 5th December, 2013.

Christopher, M. and Jüttner, U. (2000), "Supply Chain Relationships: Making the Transition to Closer Integration", *International Journal of Logistics: Research and Application*, Vol. 3, No. 1, pp. 5-23.

CIA World Factbook, (2014): The World Factbook on India. https://www.cia.gov/library/publications/the-world-factbook/geos/in.html, accessed on September 01, 2014.

Company A, interview by SDU Students, 7th October, 2013.

Cumming, B.S. (1998), "Innovation overview and future challenges", *European Journal of Innovation Management*, Vol. 1, No. 1, pp. 21-29.

Dahlman, C. and Utz, A. (2007): *Unleashing India's Innovation. Toward Sustainable and Inclusive Growth*, The World Bank, Washington DC.

Damanpour, F. (1996), "Organizational Complexity and Innovation: Developing and Testing Multiple Contingency Models", *Management Science*, Vol. 42, No. 5, pp. 693-716.

Dansk Statistik (2011), "International organisering og outsourcing", available at: http://www.dst.dk/pukora/epub/Nyt/2012/NR644.pdf, accessed 13th December, 2013.

De Mooij, M. and Hofstede, G. (2010), "The Hofstede Model - Applications to gloval branding and advertising strategy and research", *International Journal of Advertising*, Vol. 29, No. 1, pp. 85-110.

De Wit, B. and Meyer, R. (2010): *Strategy - Process, Content, Context. An International Perspective*, South-Western Cengage Learning, Hampshire.

Deloitte (2011), "Research & Development expenditure", available at: http://www.deloitte.com/assets/Dcom-India/Local%20Assets/Documents/Whitepaper_on_RD_expenditure.pdf, accessed 17th November, 2013.

Department of Science & Technology (n.d.), "Background", available at: http://www.innovationgrid.org/i3/about_innovation.html, accessed 17th November, 2013.

Department of Science & Technology (n.d.), "Objective", available at: http://www.innovationgrid.org/i3/objective.html, accessed 17th November, 2013.

Dowling, P.J., Festing, M. and Engle, A.D. (2008): *International human resource management: Managing people in a multinational context*, 5th ed., Andover, Hampshire: South-Western.

Dunning, J.H. and Lundan, S.M. (2008): *Multinational enterprises and the global economy*, 2nd ed., Edward Elgar, Cheltenham.

Dunning, J.H. (1993): *Multinational Enterprises and the Global Economy*, Addison-Wesley Publishing Company, Reading, Massachusetts

Economy Watch, 2010. India economy development. http://www.economywatch.com/indianeconomy/india-development.html, accessed on September 02, 2014.

European Commision (2013), "Research & Innovation", available at: http://ec.europa.eu/research/iscp/pdf/india_comm.pdf, accessed 17th Novemebr, 2013.

Fontes, N. (2013), "Indian WPI Inflation Rises to 14-Month High in November, available at: http://www.tradingeconomics.com/india/inflation-cpi, accessed 10th December, 2013.

Gesteland, M.R. and Gesteland, R.R. (2010): *India- Cross-Cultural Business Behavior*, Copenhagen Business School Press, Copenhagen.

Gesteland, R.R. (2005): *Cross Cultural Business Behavior - Negotiating, Selling, Sourcing and Managing Across Cultures*, 4th ed., Copenhagen Business School Press, Copenhagen.

Global Sherpa, 2014. BRIC Countries – Background, Latest News, Statistics and Original Articles. http://www.globalsherpa.org/bric-countries-brics, accessed on September 02, 2014.

Gosai, D. (2013): "History of Economic Growth in India", available at: (http://www.internationalpolicydigest.org/2013/04/24/history-of-economic-growth-in-india/, accessed 15th December, 2013.

Government of India (n.d), "Importance or Benefits", available at: http://business.gov.in/innovation/benefits.php, accesse 17th November, 2013.

Hayes, J. (2010): *The theory and practice of Change Management*, Palgrave Macmillan, New York.

Foster, C. and Heeks, R. (2013), "Conceptualising Inclusive Innovation: Modifying Systems of Innovation Frameworks to Understand Diffusion of New Technology to Low-Income Consumers", *European Journal of Development Research*, Vol. 25, No. 3, pp. 333-355.

Heeks, R. (2013), "Understanding Inclusive Development", available at: http://ict4dblog.wordpress.com/2013/08/27/understanding-inclusive-innovation/, accessed 18th November, 2013.

Ho, S.H. (2013), "India: the next produkct innovation hotbed", available at: http://scn.sap.com/community/sustainability/blog/2013/10/19/india-the-next-product-innovation-hotbed, accessed 18th November, 2013.

Hofstede, G. (1983), "National Cultures in Four Dimensions - A research-based Theory of Cultural Differences among Nations", *Int. Studies of Man. & Org.*, Vol. XIII, No. 1-2, pp. 46-74.

Hofstede, G. (1984): *Culture's Consequences - International Differences in Work-Related Values*, Abridged Edition, SAGE Publications, London

Hofstede, G. (1994): *Cultures and Organizations - Software of the Mind*, Paperback ed., HarperCollinsPublishers, London.

Hofstede, G. (2001): *Cultural Consequences - Comparing, Values, Behaviors, Institutions and Organizations Across Nations*, 2nd ed., Sage Publications, Thousand Oaks, CA.

Hofstede, G., and Hofstede, G. J. (2005): *Cultures and Organizations - Software of the Mind*, 2nd ed., McGraw-Hill, NY.

Hofstede, G. and Hofstede, G. J. (2006): *Kulturer & organisationer - Overlevelse i en grænseoverskridende verden*, 2. udgave, Handelshøjskolens Forlag, København

https://www.nationalbanken.dk/C1256BE2005737D3/side/Globaliseri ng_og_danske_direkte_investeringer/$file/KVO_08_kap4.pdf, accessed 12th December, 2013.

IFU (n.d.), "Fattige forbrugere er det nye vækstmarked", available at: http://www.ifu.dk/dk/Service/Nyheder+og+publikationer/Temaer/Te ma+om+Indien/Fattige+forbrugere+er+det+nye+v%C3%A6kstmarke d, accessed 18th November, 2013.

India Online Pages (nd), "India's Population 2013", available at: http://www.indiaonlinepages.com/population/india-current-population.html, accessed 17th November, 2013.

Innovation Council India (2010), "Introduction", available at: http://www.innovationcouncil.gov.in/index.php?option=com_content &view=article&id=26&catid=5&Itemid=5, accessed 17th November, 2013.

Jashapara, A. (2011): *Knowledge Management: An integrated Approach*, Pearson Education Limited, London.

Kaul, V. (2013), "Required: A new poverty line that shows 67% of India is poor", available at: http://firstbiz.firstpost.com/economy/required-a-new-poverty-line-that-shows-67-of-india-is-poor-43862.html, accessed 17th November, 2013.

Keeble, J. (2013), "Innovation in mobile technology drives opportunity in emerging economies", available at: http://www.theguardian.com/sustainable-business/innovation-mobile-technology-opportunity-emerging-economies, accessed 17th November, 2013.

Kotler, P., Keller, K.L., Brady, M., Goodman, M. and Hansen, T. (2010): *On competition*, Prentice Hall, London.

Kotwal, A., Ramaswami, B. and Wadhwa, W. (2011), "Economic liberalization and Indian economic growth: What's the evidence?", *Journal of Economic Literature*, Vol. 49, No. 4, pp. 1152-1199.

Law, A. (2013), "Infrastructure is India's biggest supply chain challenge", available at: http://www.thehindubusinessline.com/industry-and-economy/logistics/infrastructure-is-indias-biggest-supply-chain-challenge/article5368556.ece, accessed 13th December, 2013.

Lüthje, T. (2011), "Global production - BB", Hand-out from class.

Malhotra, Y. (2002), "Why Knowledge Management System Fail? Enablers and Constraints of Knowledge Management", in: Holsapple, C.W. (2002) (Eds.) *Handbook on Knowledge Management*, Springer-Verlag, Heidelberg.

Manyika, J., Chui, M., Bughin, J., Dobbs, R., Bisson, P. and Marrs, A. (2013): *Disruptive technologies: Advances that will transform life, business, and the global economy*, McKinsey Global Institute, May 2013, McKinsey & Company.

Maps Of India (n.d.), "India Economy", available at: http://www.mapsofindia.com/india-economy.html, accessed 18th November, 2013.

Meganathan, R. (2011), "Language policy in education and the role of English in India: From library language to language of empowerment", in Coleman, H. (2011) (Eds.) *Dreams and Realities: Developing Countries and the English Language*, The British Council, London, pp. 59-87.

Mendenhall, M.E., Dunbar, E. and Oddou, G.R. (1987), "Expatriate Selection, Training and Career-Pathing: A Review and Critique", *Human Resource Management*, Vol. 26, No. 3, pp. 331-345.

Michelsen, A.U. (2010): *Produktionsstyring: Begreber, principper og modeller*, Nyt Teknisk Forlag, København V.

Ministry of statistics and programme implementation (2013), "Energy statistics 2013", available at: http://mospi.nic.in/mospi_new/upload/Energy_Statistics_2013.pdf, accessed 12th December, 2013.

National Innovation Council (n.d.), "Innovation at Clusters", available at: http://innovation.gov.in/innovation/clusterInnovation.action, accessed 18th November, 2013.

National Innovation Foundation (n.d.), "know us", available at: http://www.nif.org.in/know_us, accessed 17th November, 2013.

OECD (1999), "OECD Benchmark definition of foreign direct investment", available at: http://www.oecd.org/dataoecd/10/16/2090148.pdf, accessed 13th December, 2013.

OECD (2013), "Country statistical profiles: Key tables from OECD", available at: http://www.oecd-ilibrary.org/economics/country-statistical-profile-india_csp-ind-table-en, accessed 5th December, 2013.

Okkels, S. (2013), "COOP fyrer og flytter job til Indien", available at: http://www.business.dk/detailhandel/coop-fyrer-og-flytter-job-til-indien, accessed 19th December, 2013.

Patankar, A. (n.d.), "Unleashing Innovations for Sustainability: An Indian Perspective", available at: http://www.innovationmanagement.se/2010/06/09/unleashing-innovations-for-sustainability-an-indian-perspective/, accessed 17th November, 2013.

Patel, R., Sethi, R., Bartz, S.E. and Israel, R. (2012), "Liberalization Of India's Foreign Direct Investment Policy On Single-Brand Retail", available at: http://www.metrocorpcounsel.com/articles/17581/liberalization-india%E2%80%99s-foreign-direct-investment-policy-single-brand-retail, accessed 17th November, 2013.

Peeters, C. (2007), "Offshoring to create value and compete for global talent", available at: http://www.solvay.edu/sites/upload/files/Offshoring/Offshoring_to_create_value.pdf, accessed 12th November, 2013.

Perumal, S. (2013), "Why study abroad?". 09 30, 2013. http://www.thehindu.com/features/education/college-and-university/why-study-abroad/article5179475.ece, accessed 17th November, 2013.

Piper, C. (2018), "Process Innovation: The crucial facilitator of product innovation", available at: http://iveybusinessjournal.com/topics/strategy/process-innovation-the-crucial-facilitator-of-product-innovation#.Uolo2tJWw6Y, accessed 18th November, 2013.

Prahalad, C.K. and Hamel, G. (1990), "The core competence of the corporation", *Harvard Business Review*, Vol. 68, No. 3, pp. 79-91.

Rajesh, S.K. (2013), "Food prices drive up Indian inflation, strengthening rate hike view", available at: http://www.reuters.com/article/2013/10/14/us-india-economy-inflation-idUSBRE99D03K20131014, accessed 18th November, 2013.

Reuters (2013), "India raises interest rates again, warns on stubborn inflation", available at: http://www.reuters.com/article/2013/10/29/us-india-economy-cbank-idUSBRE99S05V20131029, accessed 18th December, 2013.

Sanders, N.R., Locke, A., Moore, C.B. and Autry, C.W. (2007), "A Multidimensional Framework for Understanding Outsourcing Arrangements", *Journal of Supply Chain Management*, Vol. 43, No. 3, pp. 3-15.

Sanghani, P. (2009), "Knowledge Management Implementation: Holistic Framework Based on Indian Study", in *Proceedings from Pacific Asia Conference on Information Systems (PACIS 2009)*, paper 69, http://aisel.aisnet.org/pacis2009/69, Hyderabad, India.

Schumpeter, J. (1934): *The Theory of Economic Development: An Inquiry Into Profits, Capital, Credit, Interest, and the Business*, Transaction Publishers, 2008, New Brunswick, NJ.

Schumpeter, J. (1942): *Capitalism, Socialism and Democracy*, Harper & Brothers, New York, 5th ed., George Allen and Unwin, 1976, London

Soliman, F. and Spooner, K. (2000), "Strategies for implementing knowledge management: role of human resources management", *Journal of Knowledge Management*, Vol. 4, No. 4, pp. 337-345.

Srivastava, S. (2011), "A Lot of India's Innovation is Invisible, available at: http://www.forbes.com/2011/12/13/forbes-india-innovation-invisible-nirmalya-kumar-phanish-puranam.html, accessed 18th November, 2013.

Surf India (2013), "Major Industries in India", available at: http://www.surfindia.com/india-facts/major-industries-in-india.html, accessed 18th November, 2013.

Svansø, V.L. (2013), "Chr. Hansen går efter vækstmarkederne"available at: http://www.business.dk/foedevarer/chr.-hansen-gaar-efter-vaekstmarkederne, accessed 18th November, 2013.

Tamil Nadu Online (2014), "Government of Tamil Nadu: Industries department", http://www.tn.gov.in/department/16, accessed on September 01, 2014.

Taylor, G. (2013), "Implementing and maintaining a knowledge sharing culture via knowledge management teams: A shared leadership approach", *Journal of Organizational Culture, Communications and Conflict*, Vol. 17, No. 1, pp. 69-91.

The Economic Times (2010), "India ranked second in global manufacturing competence", http://articles.economictimes.indiatimes.com/2010-07-10/news/27610881_1_manufacturing-sector-manufacturing-executives-global-manufacturing-competitiveness-index, accessed on September 02, 2014.

The Economic Times (2011), "India's middle class population to touch 267 million in 5 yrs", http://articles.economictimes.indiatimes.com/2011-02-06/news/28424975_1_middle-class-households-applied-economic-research, accessed on September 01, 2014.

The Economist (2013), "India's Economy: A five-star problem", available at: http://www.economist.com/blogs/banyan/2013/08/indias-economy, accessed 18th November, 2013

The Guardian (2013), "India's trade: full list of exports, imports and partner countries", available at: http://www.theguardian.com/news/datablog/2013/feb/22/cameron-india-trade-exports-imports-partners, accessed 12th December, 2013.

The Hindu (2014), "Q1 growth has created huge positive sentiment: Modi", http://www.thehindu.com/business/gdp-growth-of-57-has-created-huge-positive-sentiment-modi/article6369662.ece?topicpage=true&topicId=1116&ref=relatedNews, accessed on September 02, 2014.

The Hindu (2014), "Most rural population now not solely in agriculture: NCAER survey", http://www.thehindu.com/news/national/most-rural-population-now-not-solely-in-agriculture-ncaer-survey/article5827481.ece, accessed on September 02, 2014.

The Hindu (2014), "India has second fastest growing services sector", http://www.thehindu.com/business/budget/india-has-second-fastest-growing-services-sector/article6193500.ece, accessed on September 02, 2014.

The Hindu (2009), "Govt launches India Innovation Initiative", *The Hindu*, 6th April, 2009.

The Hindustan Times (2014), "780 languages spoken in India, 250 died out in last 50 years", http://www.hindustantimes.com/lifestyle/books/780-languages-spoken-in-india-250-died-out-in-last-50-years/article1-1093758.aspx, accessed on September 01, 2014.

The Government of India (2013), "State of Indian Agriculture 2012-2013", http://www.agricoop.nic.in/Annual%20report2010-11/AR.pdf, accessed on September 02, 2014.

The Government of India (2014), "States and Union Territories", http://goidirectory.nic.in/state.php, accessed on September 01, 2014.

The Times of India (2013), "India to become world's most populous nation around 2028: UN", http://timesofindia.indiatimes.com/india/India-to-become-worlds-most-populous-nation-around-2028-UN/articleshow/20586377.cms, accessed on September 01, 2014.

The Times of India (2014), "New poverty line: Rs. 32 in villages, Rs. 47 in cities", http://timesofindia.indiatimes.com/india/New-poverty-line-Rs-32-in-villages-Rs-47-in-cities/articleshow/37920441.cms, accessed on September 02, 2014.

Tidd, J. and Bessant, J. (2009): *Building the Innovative Organisation*, John Wiley & Sons Ltd, West Sussex.

Trading Economics (2013), "India Gross National Product", available at: http://www.tradingeconomics.com/india/gross-national-product, accessed 18th November, 2013.

TRAI (2012), "Telecom Regulatory Authority of India", available at: http://www.trai.gov.in/WriteReadData/WhatsNew/Documents/PR-TSD-Mar03052012.pdf, accessed 17th November, 2013.

Transparency International (2013), "Corruption Perception Index 2013", available at: http://cpi.transparency.org/cpi2013/results/, accessed 17th December, 2013.

Tung, R.L. (1981), "Selection and training of personnel for overseas assignments", *Columbia Journal of World Business*, Vol. 16, No. 1, pp. 68-79.

Udenrigsministeriet (2011), "Vækstmarkedsstrategier", available at: http://um.dk/da/~/media/UM/Danish-site/Documents/Eksportraadet/Markeder/BRIK/100718_UM_Indien_3.pdf, accessed 17th November, 2013.

Udenrigsministeriet (2012), "Vækstmarkedsstrategi – Indien", available at: http://www.evm.dk/~/media/oem/pdf/2012/pressemeddelelser-2012/09-05-12-vaekstmarkedsstrategier-brik/indien.ashx, accessed 10th December, 2013.

Udenrigsministeriet (2013), "Fakta om Indien", available at: http://indien.um.dk/da/her-arbejder-vi/, accessed 13th December, 2013.

WHO (2013), "Trade, foreign policy, diplomacy and health", available at: http://www.who.int/trade/glossary/story043/en/, accessed 13th December, 2013.

World Inflation Data (2014), "Inflation India – current Indian inflation", http://www.inflation.eu/inflation-rates/india/inflation-india.aspx, accessed on September 02, 2014.

Index

4P framework; 56
Absorptive capacity; 100
Affective value; 88
Brazilian culture; 143
Butterfly approach; 101
BWE; 13
Caresoft; 13
Christopher Rajkumar; 14
Codification strategy; 103
Cognitive value; 88
Collectivism; 33
Content Management System; 105
Creative climate; 76
Cultural learning; 144
Culture; 25
Customer Relationship Management; 106
Danfoss; 13
Data mining; 105
Data warehouse; 105
Deal-focused; 35
Department of Entrepreneurship and Relationship Management; 11
Diamond approach; 101
Economic value; 88
El-Forge; 13
Enterprise Resource Planning; 105
Expatriate; 98
Explicit knowledge; 89
Femininity; 40
Flat hierarchy; 100
FLSmidth; 13
Foreign Direct Investment; 53
Globalisation; 113
Horizontal communication; 100
Impressive experiences; 140
Inclusive innovation; 67
Incremental improvements; 56
India Innovation Portal; 59
Indian business culture; 145
Individualism; 33
Ingeborg Uldahl; 14
Innovation; 53
Innovation drivers; 57
Kaizen box; 31
Knowledge Management; 83
Location-specific advantages; 116
Long term orientation; 43
Masculinity; 40
Mohandas Gandhi; 18
Monochronic time behaviour; 45
Most impressive experiences; 140
Moustache; 48
MSc line in Business Controlling; 13
MSc line in International Business Development; 12
MSc line in Management and Leadership; 12
Nod; 48
Offshoring; 114
Ole Kirks Fond; 14
OLI; 115
Outsourcing; 114
Ownership-specific advantages; 116
Paradigm innovation; 66
PDCA Wheel; 109
PESTEL analysis; 124
Physical value; 88
Political value; 88
Polychronic time behaviour; 45
Power distance; 29
Process innovation; 64
Product innovation; 65

Radical changes; 56
Rambøll; 13
Ramsay'; 13
Relationship-focused; 35
Religion; 21
Religion in India; 21
SDCA Wheel; 110
Short term orientation; 43
Social value; 88
Tacit knowledge; 85
The Danish Consulate in Chennai; 14
Tresu Production Systems A/S; 14
Uncertainty avoidance; 37
University Press of Southern Denmark; 12
Vestas; 13

About the Editors

Jan Stentoft, PhD, is a Professor in Supply Chain Management (SCM) at the Department of Entrepreneurship and Relationship Management, University of Southern Denmark, Kolding. His research and teaching areas are within Supply Chain Management, Supply Chain Innovation, Enterprise Resource Planning, and Corporate Social Responsibility. He has practical industry experience from positions as Director (Programme Management Office) at LEGO Systems A/S, Axapta, ERP Project Manager at Gumlink A/S, and as management consultant in a wide number of industrial enterprises from his own consulting practice.

Ole Stegmann Mikkelsen, PhD, is am Assistant Professor in Supply Chain Management (SCM) at the Department of Entrepreneurship and Relationship Management, University of Southern Denmark, Kolding. His research and teaching areas are within Supply Chain Management, Global Sourcing, Strategic Sourcing and Corporate Social Responsibility. He has published both nationally and internationally and has practical industrial experience from positions as Purchaser/Planner from Milliken Denmark A/S, and Strategic Purchasing Consultant and Director (Group Procurement Development and Support/finance) at Danfoss A/S.

Antony Paulraj, PhD, is the Globalisation Professor of Supply Chain Management (SCM) at the Department of Entrepreneurship and Relationship Management, University of Southern Denmark, Kolding. His research and teaching areas are within Supply Chain Management, Strategic Buyer-Supplier Relationships, Strategic Sourcing, Sustainable Supply Chain Management, and Supply Chain Innovation. He has published extensively in leading international peer-reviewed operations and supply chain management journals. He also has extensive practical industry experience from positions as Senior Information Technology Consultant at TekSystems, Inc., Ohio, USA, and Technical Consultant at Information Control Corporation, Ohio, USA.

Previous field study projects

Arlbjørn, J.S. & Mikkelsen, O.S. (Eds.) (2013) *Doing Business in China: Report from a Field Study Trip*, University Press Southern Denmark, Odense.

Arlbjørn, J.S. & de Haas, H. (Eds.) (2011) *Supply Chain Management: Brazil as an Emergent Economy*, University Press Southern Denmark, Odense.

Arlbjørn, J.S, de Haas, H. Ingstrup, M.B. & van Liempd, D. (Eds.) (2010) *Supply Chain Management: Business Operations in India*, University Press Southern Denmark, Odense.

Arlbjørn, J.S. & de Haas, H. (Eds.) (2009) *Supply Chain Management: Issues to consider when doing business in China*, Academica, Aarhus.